THE RISE OF THE
FOURTH POLITICAL THEORY

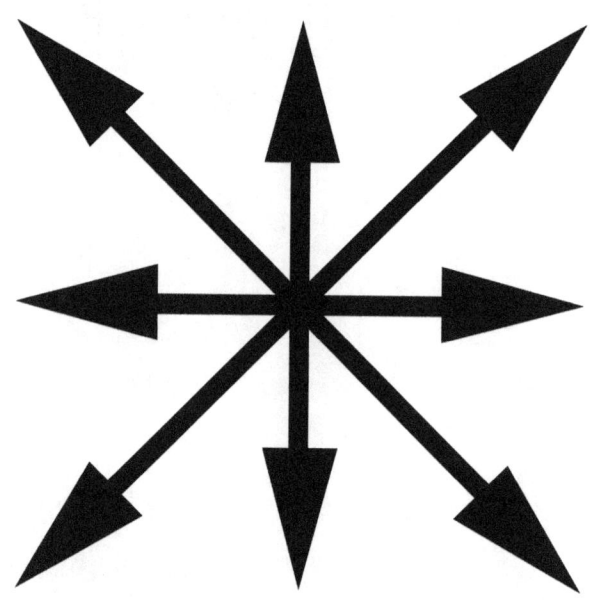

THE
RISE OF THE
FOURTH
POLITICAL
THEORY

ALEXANDER DUGIN

The Fourth Political Theory vol. II

ARKTOS
LONDON 2017

Arktos.com fb.com/Arktos @arktosmedia arktosmedia

Copyright © 2017 by Arktos Media Ltd.

All rights reserved. No part of this book may be reproduced or utilised in any form or by any means (whether electronic or mechanical), including photocopying, recording or by any information storage and retrieval system, without permission in writing from the publisher.

ISBN
978-1-917646-26-0 (Paperback)
978-1-912079-54-4 (Hardback)
978-1-912079-53-7 (Ebook)

Translation
Michael Millerman

Editing
Jason Reza Jorjani

Layout & Cover
Tor Westman

CONTENTS

PART I. DEMOCRACY AND CONSERVATISM

1. Democracy: Sacred or Secular? 1
   Democracy as an Archaic Phenomenon: Collective Ecstasy 1
   Democracy is Founded on Inequality, "*Idiotes*" 2
   Political Modernization: From Democracy to Tyranny 3
   The Paradox of the Renaissance: Forward to Antiquity 4
   Archaic Signs of Modern Democracies: Suffragists and Hitler 5
   Global Democracy as the Kingdom of the Anti-Christ 6

2. Conservatism as a Project and Episteme 7
   The Inadequacy of Common Presentations of Conservatism 7
   The Philosophy of History and Diachronism 7
   The Conservative and the Constant 8
   Being is More Primary Than Time 9
   The Conservative Project and Its Metaphysics 10
   The Coming-to-be and the Coming-forth in Christian Eschatology 11
   The Conservative Project Against Technology 12
   The Conservative Episteme 13
   Humanism as a Weapon of the Conservative 14
   Empire — A Big Man 15
   The Trichotomy of Empire 16
   The Value of War 17
   The Tripartite Structure of the Conservative Episteme 18

PART II. EMPIRE AND THE EURASIAN IDEA

3. The West and its Challenge 21
   What Do We Understand By "The West"? 21
   Europe and Modernity 22
   The Idea of "Progress" as the Basis for Political Colonization
   and Cultural Racism 23

The Archaic Roots of Western Exclusiveness 24
Empire and its Influence on Contemporary Westernization. 25
Modernization: Endogenous and Exogenous 26
Two Types of Society with Exogenous Modernization. 28
The Conception of "West" and "East" in the Yalta World 31
In the 1990s "the West" Becomes Globalization 34
Globalization 36
Post-Modernity and "the West" 37
The Post-West 39
The Gap Between the Theory and Practice of Globalism 40
USA and the EU: The Two Poles of the Western World at
the Start of the 21st Century 42
The Identity of Russia: Country or...?. 44
Russia as a Civilization (Cultural-Historical Type) 48
Russia and the West in the 1990s 50
The Strategy of "World Government" in Relation to
the USSR and Russia 53
Russia and the West in the Putin Era. 55
Challenge to the West 56
CFR Networks in the Putin Period. 58
Relations of Russia and the West in the Future. 59
Perestroika 2: Russia Integrates into the Global "West" 60
Russia and the West in Eurasian Theory 64
Russia and the West From the Perspective of
the Contemporary Russian Government. 68
The Subjective Position of the Author 70

4. Carl Schmitt's Principle of "Empire" and
   the Fourth Political Theory. 72
   The Order of "Large Spaces" 72
   The Monroe Doctrine 73
   The Juridical Status of the Monroe Doctrine: Politics and
   the Law, Legality and Legitimacy. 75

    The Evolution of the "Monroe Doctrine"............................76
    The Large Space and *"Reich"* in Schmitt's Understanding..............79
    The Soviet "Large Space" or Russian *Reich* 83
    The New Relevance of the Fourth Political Theory...................84

5. **The Project "Empire"** 88
    Empire without an Emperor 88
    Empire as the Optimal Instrument for the Making of Civil Society 88
    The Definition of Empire...89
    The Empire of the Neo-Cons (Benevolent Empire) 90
    Negri and Hardt's Criticism of "Empire"............................92
    Alternatives to Global Empire: The Extension of
    the Yalta-Based Status Quo...93
    The Islamic Empire (The Global Caliphate) 95
    The European Union: A Teetering Empire 97
    Russian "Defeatists"...98
    The Anti-Imperialist Supporters of Russian Sovereignty..............99
    The Eurasianist Empire of the Future 102
    CIS — The Site of the Future Empire 103
    Empire After Tskhinvali 105
    Friendly Empire — The Eurasian Axis 108
    Eurasianism as an Imperial Ideology...............................110

6. **Eurasianism (A Political Poem)** 113
    Eurasianism as Philosophy (What is Philosophy?)...................113
    The *Narod* is Love...114
    The Russian Body..115
    The Gift of Language 116
    A Russian Falls Asleep and Awakens................................117
    The Russian Person as an Absolute.................................118
    The *Narod's* Borders 118
    State-Hedgehog..120
    The Spirit of the Earth 121
    Territorial Space as a Form of Life 121

Living Borders 122

The Serbian Mountain 123

Eternity in Your Palms 124

There is No Time 125

For the Absolute Against the Relative 125

The Absolute Motherland 126

Russia is an Ontological Concept 127

The Individualization of Supra-Individual Experience 127

The Ontological Map of the World (Suhrawardi) 127

The Wellsprings of Western Exile 128

The Journey to the Country of the East 129

The Integration of the West into Eurasia (Descent into Hell) 129

The Purple Archangel of Russia 130

Spiritual Teaching: The Call to Repentance 131

Eurasian Truth 132

Eurasian Analysis 132

The Eurasian Language 133

The Eurasian Forecast 133

Eurasian Discipline is the Root of Freedom 133

Atlanticism is Absolute Evil 134

MTV — The Personification of the Abomination of Desolation:
The Imperative of Relaxation 135

The Entropic Ontology of the Far West (Behind the
Pillars of Hercules) 136

Polarity of Signs 137

The Problem of the "I" 138

A Name is Serious 139

The Heresy of Individualism 140

Man is Simply a Conditionality 140

The Imperative of Struggle 141

We are Going Beyond the Horizon 141

Grass Through Asphalt 142

The Eurasian Ark 142

The Eurasian Network 143

Of Eurasian Affairs 143

A Simplification of Eurasianism 144

The Attraction of Allies 145

Eurasian Strength 145

Eurasian Goals 146

Part III. The Russian Behemoth

7. The Structure of Russia's Sociogenesis 149

　The Formula of Russia's Sociogenesis: Constants and Variables 149

　Clarification of the Constants 150

　Clarification of the Variables 152

　Varieties of States 153

　Varieties of Society 157

　The Political-Economic Forms are Irrelevant 157

　The Russian Axis 158

　Russia's Ethnic Core — the Russian *Narod* — Russian Civilization 158

　The Russian Axis of Constants 158

　Civilization and Government 159

　The Fraction Society/*Narod* 160

　Sociogenesis and the Analysis of Present Russian Society 161

　The Contradiction Between the Constants and the Variables
　in Today's Russia 162

　"The Party of the Constants" and "The Party of the Variables" 164

　A Forecast of Russia's Future Social System 165

8. The Russian Leviathan (State Terror) .167

　Fear as Trembling 167

　Hobbes and His Monster 168

　"The Russian Behemoth" 170

　Why is there Repression? Four Main Principles 171

　The Proportions of Fear in Various Stages of Russian History 177

A Digression on The Freedom Loving and Recalcitrant
Russian *Narod*. 178
"The Russian Leviathan" Today 179
What Should We Do?. 182
There Are — There Cannot Fail to Be — Ways Out 182

9. Questioning Modernization 185
10. Interests and Values After Tskhinvali 194
Revival of the Debate. 194
Interests and Rules. 195
From Interests to Values 196
The US Declared Its Interests Universal Values 197
Western Values Are Not Universal; Different Peoples
Have Other Values 198
Russia is not a European Country, but a Eurasian Civilization 199
Tskhinvali Put an End to the Debate about Values. 200
We Defended Our Values — Hence, We're Right 202
We Defended Our Interests — Hence, We Are Strong 204
The End of Westernism in Russia. 205

Appendixes

Alexander Dugin on Martin Heidegger 209
The Four Political Theories 224

PART I
DEMOCRACY AND CONSERVATISM

CHAPTER 1

Democracy: Sacred or Secular?

In relation to democracy, there exist a multitude of erroneous myths. Most people are certain that this is the most contemporary, developed, "civilized" form of political organization, founded on the principle of the political equality of all individuals in a concrete society. To put it mildly, this is not at all so.

Democracy as an Archaic Phenomenon: Collective Ecstasy

Democracy is the most ancient, archaic, primitive and, if you prefer, "barbarian" form of political organization. The most ancient societies known to us from history were built on precisely the democratic principle. The main decisions relating to the fate of the tribe or even to the entire *ethnos* were always adopted collectively, on the basis of the general opinion of the plenipotentiary members of the society. The oldest families, soldiers, priests, and those called the "masters of fire" (household proprietors) comprised the elementary "parliament" of ancient peoples. Among the Germans this was called *"Ting"*; among the Slavs, *"Veche"*; even the Roman expression *"Res Publica"* recalls the ancient collective assemblies of Latin tribes, where the general "things" fundamental for life had been discussed (*"res"* in Latin is "thing," which is close in sense to the Russian "*Veche*" or German "*ting*" or "*ding*," in German, also "thing").

At the basis of democracy lies the principle of the collective form of decision making, and this procedure must take into account the widest possible spectrum of representatives from society. But this very principle is an inalienable part of ancient, archaic societies, where the individual has not yet been separated out as a self-reliant (independent) quantity and the most important historical actor was "the soul of the *ethnos*," most often understood as a "totem," "spirit," or "ethnic deity." It was precisely in order to allow this supra-individual authority to interfere directly in the fate of the collective that democratic procedures were introduced. There was a demand to come to a decision about "things" (*veche*), which none of the participants could do separately. This decision was anticipated from a "transcendental" authority, which manifested itself through the assembly. For that reason, all assemblies opened with rituals during which gods and spirits were summoned. In fact, it was they, acting through people, who made the decisions. That is the literal meaning of the Roman saying "*Vox populi — vox Dei*" the voice of the people is the voice of the divine.

Thus, at the basis of democracy lies the archaic mysticism of collective ecstasy, when the community "leaves" itself to meet the collective soul ("God"), which, on the other hand, "comes" to them.

Democracy is Founded on Inequality, "*Idiotes*"

Democracy does not recognize individual equality. There is a cruel quality in it, separating those who are admitted to participate in "the political ecstasy of decision" from those who are not. For that reason, the real participants of democratic procedures in all societies recognized only concrete social groups. The structures differed in different societies, but the principle of the inclusion of some into the democratic process and the exclusion of others from it is the fundamental sign of all types of democracy.

In German warrior tribes, only free warriors and priests were admitted to the "*ting.*" But since practically all the members of these tribes (including the priests) were warriors, the German warrior democracy, understandably, was the widest and most direct. Only slaves of war were excluded, along with women, children, and, naturally, foreigners. In the Greek *polis* where the democratic model was established, as in Athens, for instance, in order to participate in democracy it was necessary to be a "citizen" of the *polis*, which required the elevation of one's family to the mythological fountainhead of the *polis* (the nobility), the possession of a certain level of material goods, and compliance with some determinate moral cast of mind. Poor folk, slaves and women were likewise excluded from democratic procedures, and the "foreign born," including nobility from another *polis*, were called "*idiotes*" (Gk: "excluded ones," "non-citizens"). Underlying the contemporary clinical term "idiot" is the political notion, designating a person kept strictly apart from democratic participation.

In all types of democracy a selection of its lawful participants is done to ensure the unconstrained access of "the soul" ("God," "the gods") of the collective to involve itself in the fate of the society.

Political Modernization: From Democracy to Tyranny

In the history of the West as in some other civilizations, the modernization of political systems proceeded from a rejection of democracy, most often in favor of aristocracy and monarchy. Although even in this case the sacred character of power was preserved, the individual, rational principle became increasingly visible. Political decisions were now made to a large degree by individuals or by a separate individual and therefore acquired a more rational and purely human character. In moving away from archaic democracy, civilization shunned the proximity of the gods and the world in which the human and the godly intertwined to the point of being indistinguishable. Thus, Aristotle wrote that, "Democracy is pregnant with tyranny." Tyranny supersedes democracy as a more modern kind of political organization, where, for the first time, the separate individual is clearly revealed, in our case, the tyrant. In this process, the "divine" is humanized.

The Paradox of the Renaissance: Forward to Antiquity

How then can we understand the fact that in the modern age, in the era of the Enlightenment and progress, Europe turned precisely to democracy, the traces of which were lost in Western societies over two thousand years ago? It does indeed seem that between the ancient democracy of Athens and the modern European parliamentary republics, many centuries of Western history were marked by monarchic-aristocratic political systems. The answer is rooted in the Renaissance era.

The Renaissance era is responsible for many paradoxes that later made themselves known. In that period, a European genius decided to cast off the rational norms of the scholastics and to liberate the human dimension. Usually this is construed as a step forward. Few pay attention to the fact that the figures of the Renaissance themselves took as a model precisely the ancient Platonic man and repudiated Catholic dogmas not for the sake of a secular, scientific order (which did not yet exist) but for magical, alchemical, and hermetic teachings. In other words, they were favoring deep, archaic knowledge, the ecstatic practice of experiencing the all-encompassing, sacred character of the world. Marsilio Ficino, Giordano Bruno, and Michelangelo were passionate advocates of Platonism and ancient Greece, searchers of the Egyptian mysteries, and connoisseurs of Kabbalah. The European interest in democracy stems from this heritage. Political democracy was discovered together with Plotinus and Hermes Trismegistus, the philosopher's stone, and the ancient gods who seemed to have left the world forever.

Archaic Signs of Modern Democracies: Suffragists and Hitler

That is why we encounter upsurges here and there of the archaic principle in recent European history. Democracy itself becomes something "sacred." Simply try in a conversation with a typical, modern European or American to doubt democracy — you'll see the result. You'll become an "outcast," a "non-citizen," an "*idiotes*." This can seem strange to many today, but women in Western societies were given the right to vote only after three centuries had elapsed since democratic procedures were introduced in Europe. At the end of the 19th and beginning of the 20th century, the "suffragists" (from the French word meaning: "voting") demanded "that European women be permitted to vote equally with men." Over a hundred years ago, American democracy still involved a racial principle (the rights of native Americans and of African slaves were curtailed) and property qualification (the presence of considerable property), which limited the circle of "the elect" permitted to exercise democracy. The American political system included the wide activities of masonic lodges and other secret societies, which gave, and continue to give, American democracy its "sacred" content. And, finally, a completely paradoxical example: the establishment of Nazi Germany. How did it happen that in a developed, modern, civilized and enlightened European country of the 20th century — a century of civilization and progress — on the basis of an absolutely democratic procedure, with widespread popular approval, a man came to power who reestablished in Germany not a medieval, but an even more archaic spirit, with mass rituals, irrational pseudo-scientific research, and harsh racial segregation? Here, as with all democracies, the principle of "separation" was displayed anew in full measure: some were admitted to the ecstatic practice, and others were cruelly removed from it.

Global Democracy as the Kingdom of the Anti-Christ

21st century democracy presents itself externally as the most modern political system and attempts to include all individuals, without respect to citizenship, sexual orientation, material capability, or racial and ethnic specifics. It is based on a theory of "human rights." But in this case, too, there is no trace of either the rationality of elections, the significance of individuality, or the equality of influence on decision-making. The reasonableness of one person is suppressed by the unreasonableness of another, and through all the attempts to "modernize" democracy its ancient, absolutely archaic and in the final analysis irrational essence (what "rationality" is there in the turn to the vague, ecstatic "spirit"?!) emerges again and again. Only now, through the project of worldwide civil society, there speaks not the spirit of the *polis*, tribe or *narod* [*Volk*, people. Most often transliterated in the singular as a technical term and translated "peoples" when plural. The adjectival form has been translated "popular" or "ethnosocial" depending on context], but some other kind of "generalized," "common" essence, which the Christian tradition is inclined to interpret as "the Prince of the World." And the inarticulate mumbling of the planetary masses is interpreted by the colleges of the ancient high priests, who speak today in the masks of champions of "the open society" or "globalization." One can guess whom they really serve.

CHAPTER 2

Conservatism as a Project and Episteme

The Inadequacy of Common Presentations of Conservatism

One of the most typical delusions regarding the concept of "conservatism" consists in the simplistic idea that conservatives are those, who "want to preserve the past, leaving (or making) everything as it was." In fact, in the political sense, conservatism is not the preservation of the past and not even the appeal to tradition. Conservatism is a philosophical approach, which interprets time very specifically. It does not merely select some sector of time (the past) as a priority, but operates with a peculiar notion of time, which is by no means banal and which demands more careful examination.

The Philosophy of History and Diachronism

In the culture of modernity we have become used to operating with a diachronic approach to history, which has become for us something self-evident. This approach isolates three temporal categories, set in strict and irreversible order: the past, the present ("the passing"), and the future. Notice, "the past" is that which "has passed." The present is that which "stands" [the Russian noun for "present," *nastoyashcheye*, consists of the prefix *na-* "on" and the root *stoyat'*, "to stand] and the future is that which will come, or come forth. The roots of all these concepts—the past, present and future—are tied [in Russian] not to the sense of being, but to the sense of movement (or its moment of "standing," "stopping on.") The specific character of historicism and the philosophical of history consist in precisely this. This model of understanding the world through movement and stillness was proposed in the West in modernity [the Russian term for "modernity" is "New Time"] together with the concept of progress. Such unidirectional time already contains in itself the idea of pro-gress [from the Latin *progressus*], that is, literally, "movement forward."

The total and extensive adoption of this diachronic paradigm at times forces conservatives themselves to direct their attention to the past as normative when laying out their philosophical and political positions. The conservative thereby as it were agrees with linear time. He acknowledges the fact of progress, but only to extract from it an alternative, negative conclusion. It looks like in acting in this way the conservative is by definition retrograde, that is, someone who "goes back." But that is incorrect; because it is not at all what has passed that interests the conservative, especially as modern people understand this "past."

The Conservative and the Constant

In fact, in place of a temporal diachronic topography of past, present, and future, conservatives operate with an entirely different, non-diachronic, synchronic model. The conservative protects and defends not the past but the constant, the perennial, that which essentially always remains identical to itself. Defining conservatism, the philosopher Alain de Benoist said very truly that, "the root is not that which once was, but that which always grows," something living.

As soon as we affirm that conservatives do not fight for the past, but rather for the constant, for the fundamental constants of society, humanity and the soul, we will be able on good grounds to understand the attitude of the conservative toward all three temporal modalities. Like the present and the future, the past is valuable not in itself, but only in the fact that there is something constant in it.

There are many periods in Russian history differing in substance and significance, and all of them are in the past. In the past were the Specific Fragmentation, the Mongolian Conquest, the Times of Trouble, the Dissidence, the Petrine Reforms, the Bironovshchina, the February Revolution, Khrushchev's Thaw, Perestroika, Yeltsinism and much more that is categorically unacceptable and anomalous for a consistent Russian conservative. When a conservative turns over the pages of a book of Russian history, he sees in it both golden and abominable pages. What is common to them is only that they are written in blood.

Being is More Primary Than Time

The conservative strives to understand what in the historical process of a concrete narod [people] — in our case, Russia — was constant and invariable, what of that exists now, and what, correspondingly, will be in the future. But the most important idea of conservatism is that it thinks not about the past but about what has been, not about the present but about that which is right now, not about that which will come, but about that which will be realized, which will be [note: the distinction is between words that indicate movement or its lack, on one hand, and those linked with forms of the verb to be, on the other].

Here it is entirely appropriate to appeal to Heidegger's philosophical model, centered on the question of being. If for "progressives" and the followers of the philosophy of history being is a function of becoming (of history, time), then for the conservative (Heidegger himself was a complete conservative, moreover, a conservative revolutionary) time (history, duration, *Zeit*) is a function of being. Being is primary, time is secondary.

This signifies a great deal. The secret of conservatism lies herein. That which appertains to being surpasses time and does not depend on time. For that reason, that which really was surely is now and will be tomorrow. Moreover, that which will be tomorrow surely was yesterday and is today, inasmuch as time does not rule over being. On the contrary, being rules over time and predetermines its structure, its course, its substance. It is precisely this that makes possible the conservative's position not only in respect to the past and the present, but in respect to what will be. With this, the possibility of the existence of the conservative project is justified.

The Conservative Project and Its Metaphysics

The conservative project is a grasping for the concentration point of being in the future and an orientating of social, cultural and political energies around that point. For the conservative that point is not a conventional or arbitrary fancy. It is already absolutely real for him here and now. The conservative does not play with probabilities: he knows what he is doing and knows what will be.

The significance of the conservative project is that it is secured by being itself, by philosophy itself (conservative philosophy), which places being above time. The conservative not only expects the future, he builds it, he brings it into effect; he brings about its presence on the foundation of his increased attention to being.

This increased attention to being can show itself as love for the past, as well as for what has been. In this case the past is apprehended as being-present, utterly real, not only indirectly touching reality, but constituting its essence, making it that which it is. The conservative sees the eternal in the past and only for that reason does it stand out for him as a normative for the present and the future. This is the eternal past that lasts here and now. It conceals itself from the superficial glance of the modernist (Heraclitus said long ago that "nature loves to hide") but it discloses itself to him who harkens to the quiet voice of being.

But the conservative can also be one who is completely indifferent to the past, but who strives to grab hold of being in a direct and actual existential experience, most often through horror and other special operations of metaphysics. If being reveals itself in the present through phenomenological presence, it will also appear in the past, since the past, without any kind of preliminary deliberation, will reveal itself as what has been; that is, as the actual.

And finally, a conservative can be primarily concentrated on the future, on the sphere of the project. In this case, too, he will not give up his principles in the least. Striving to realize in the coming-forward the coming-to-be [the first term is the Russian word for "future" linked to the sense of movement, the second term is the term for future linked to being], he constitutes there — if the project is successful — being in its a-temporal aspect; that is, he will reveal the essence of the present and will receive the key to the ontological deciphering of the past.

In this way, the conservative project can be the secondary or primary care of the conservative, but in any case it is always possible and even inevitable, inasmuch as the full-fledged conservative approach to the world and history contains the ontological dimension of the coming-forth — that is, the figure of the coming-to-be [see previous note].

The Coming-to-be and the Coming-forth in Christian Eschatology

Conservatives are often (though not always) religious people. This is logical: studying eternity, they do not have grounds for disbelieving religion. After all, eternity is that which interests conservatives above all. The German philosopher Arthur Moeller van den Bruck said along these lines: "Eternity is on the side of the conservative."

Russian conservatism is naturally founded on Orthodoxy. The sphere of Christian teachings depicting the coming-to-be (the end of times) is called "eschatology." In Christian teaching, eschatological pessimism and eschatological optimism co-exist. The orthodox know that in the coming-forth the Anti-Christ will come (come forth); but they also know that he will be defeated by Christ in his glorious and terrible Second Coming.

This duality is important for the very structure of the conservative project. It is necessarily dual and dramatic, at once pessimistic and optimistic. The conservative project sees suffering, anxiety, horror, fear, adversity and catastrophes ahead. However, it also sees triumph, victory, the descent to Earth of the Heavenly Jerusalem, the universal revealing of eternity and the abolition of death. The task of the conservative, defending eternity, is to change the coming-forth in favor of the coming-to-be or to fight on the side of the coming-to-be against the coming-forth. The Anti-Christ is coming forth, but the Second Coming will be.

The Conservative Project Against Technology

The initiation of the conservative project in contemporary Russian society, of course, must not, by any means or under any circumstances, flirt with technology, with expert packaging, with glamour, with simulacra. The conservative project must not allure, tempt, or fascinate anyone. It must reveal the truth. It may frighten, inasmuch as it calls things by their own names, presents the situation as it is, and describes it adequately.

As soon as conservatives will be able to clarify that they are not defending the past, but rather the constant, the serious development of the conservative project will begin. All the conservative projects that exist today in Russia, despite their other accomplishments, are methodologically, conceptually and philosophically on the wane, weak and superficial. They lack the most important thing: the breath of eternity.

They are too much like the opportunistic and ephemeral phenomena against which they propose to struggle. Technological conservatism is a deliberate simulacrum.

That the government does not hurry to act in a conservative manner is in part explained by the fact that contemporary Russian conservatives, imitating the liberal style, attempt to impart to conservative ideas a catchy and marketable package. But this contradicts the very essence of conservatism, and so the result is something misshapen and repulsive. The government, which as it is trusts nothing and no one (now and then one receives the impression that it does not even trust itself), feels in such an approach banal political and even clan interests, an attempt to influence, or, what is worse, to seize power, and so it immediately throws these projects aside as irrelevant. Moreover, it is not important that the government reproaches the conservatives for their insufficient technological effectiveness. By this criterion, conservatism will always yield to liberalism, as that very criterion is liberal. Conservatism can and must take a different path — the demonstration of the irresistible truth of eternity and a concentrated will to show this by any means and at any price. Eternity at any price.

The Conservative Episteme

The inability in contemporary Russia of formulating the conservative project is not an accidental thing. We have a fundamental epistemological deficit, which is connected with the results of Soviet influence and the consequent liberal wave in the humanities and social sciences. Both communism and liberalism are founded on the primacy of time over being and suppose that all reality is becoming. The communists have some distant likeness to the ontology of the coming-to-be; liberalism is pragmatic, eclectic, and phenomenological, bracketing being, and contenting itself with the ephemeral and the momentary. But in both cases the scientific matrix is built on the explicit negation of eternity. But this cannot but affect the whole system of the humanities, including, maybe even above all, education.

In this way, the epistemological deficit has a structural character. It does not come down to our lacking conservative minds and adequate research studies. We are lacking the episteme.

For the development of full-fledged conservative thought, a preliminary system of coordinates is necessary, a sort of new, expressly conservative (ideologically, not methodologically) sociology, which is ready to perform the gigantic work of making broad revisions to our scientific, humanitarian and sociological conceptions. Only after this work of producing a conservative episteme can one speak of the appearance of a conservative project. Its delegation to the government will then be a secondary question. If conservatism establishes itself ontologically, one will be able to raise the question of its political implementation. But where this becomes possible, society itself will be different. What parties or personalities will pick it up, how they will popularize it, and, moreover, realize it, is the tenth matter of business. While it doesn't exist, and the epistemological prerequisites are lacking, it is useless to guess about these things. In this case we sink into simulacra anew.

Humanism as a Weapon of the Conservative

In contrast to the habitual attacks on humanism by the conservatives of the past, Heidegger, for instance, did not hesitate to attend to it. This is revealing. Conservatism, defending eternity, defends also the eternity of man, man as eternity, man as structure, provided with invariable attributes and inalienable life. Man [i.e. the human being, not man as opposed to woman] is a conservative concept. He was before, he is now, and he must be in the coming-to-be. What changes in man is secondary for the conservative. What is principle in him is that which remains invariable.

Steadiest in man are his dreams, his reveries, his wishes, the deep movements of his soul. Man is dynamic on the surface of his consciousness; in the depths, in his unconscious, he is static and lives outside of time. The subjects of dreams do not change, the sheaths do. Plane, train and rocket are essentially an expression of the dream about eternal angels and magical runners.

The conservative must be on the side of man as something invariable — something paradoxical and contradictory, fine, but rooted in being, and what is more, in a different way than everything else is rooted in it. Heidegger called this difference, fundamental for his philosophy, "*Dasein.*" Christianity talks of the "New Man," whose nature is illuminated by the Incarnation, the Resurrection and the Ascension.

But the conservative, in contrast to communists and liberals, does not stand on the side of "the little man" (in all senses); he fights for "the big man," for "*homo maximus.*" The conservative everywhere loves the great, and he loves the great and the lofty in man.

Man, in his "maximally humanitarian" understanding, is regarded as a mediator between Heaven and Earth. He strives to incarnate in himself the contrasts of the world: the high and the low, love and death, ecstasy and suffering, life and soul, flesh and divinity. The conservative acts under the banner of such a man.

Empire — A Big Man

As in anthropology the philosophy of conservatism is oriented toward the maximum scale, so in society and in politics conservatism loves everything great, gigantic, boundless and endless. For that reason, as a rule, conservatives are supporters of Empire. There is a direct homology between Empire and "the big man" (*homo maximus*). Empire is the maximal society, the greatest possible scale of government. Empire also embodies the confluence of Heaven and Earth, the combination into unity of differences, which, preserving themselves as such, are integrated into a general strategic matrix. Empire is the highest form of humanity, its highest manifestation. There is nothing more humane than Empire.

Empire is the horizon of man, the horizon of society toward which it strives, proceeding through integration and generalization. Empire realizes in itself ontological wholeness, the flourishing of being. Thus, Empire is always sacred, sacral. It is no accident that in Byzantium and Russia there emerged a deep alliance between the Empire and the Church. Hence the symphony of powers and the horizon of religious belief connected with the idea of Empire, Kingdom. For the conservative, Empire is the highest, inherently self-sufficient ontological value.

The Trichotomy of Empire

In its most general features, the conservative project must be trichotomous. One of two classical anthropologies in the Christian tradition — in particular, the anthropology of the blessed apostle Paul — is trichotomous, distinguishing in man spirit, body, and soul. This trichotomy is also fully applicable to the structure of the ideal Empire. It is formulated with regard to Empire in the following way: territorial space, *narod* [*Volk*, people. Most often transliterated in the singular as a technical term and translated "peoples" when plural. The adjectival form has been translated "popular" or "ethnosocial" depending on context. Dugin discusses the category of *narod* in detail in his book *Ethnosociology*], and religion.

Territorial space, ground, zones of control and influence — this is the corporal substance of Empire, and it corresponds to the body in man. The limitlessness and breadth of Russian spatiality is the visible expression of the large scale of the Russian *homo maximus*. Empire is corporeal, but its body is sacral; hence, the concern for the native soil, for the Motherland, the Fatherland, the Commonwealth.

The *narod* corresponds to the soul: it lives and moves, loves and hates, falls and lifts itself up anew, takes flight and suffers. It is dual, at times pretending to be negligible, but occasionally opening up the treasure of its own being. It is alive, the sacred *narod*, the *narod* of soul. Religion pertains to the spirit. It reveals celestial perspectives, secures contact with eternity, and directs the gaze to Heaven. As man necessarily has a body, soul, and spirit, according to Christianity, so Empire has a territorial space, *narod* and religion.

The Value of War

Conservatives are rarely pacifists. Among us, it has become commonplace to praise peace and fight for it. True, the more they talk of peace, the more the blood flows and the innocent suffer. Here, the conservative must not lie: he prefers war, not peace. Nietzsche was not afraid in his time to exclaim: "love war more than peace, and short peace more than long!"

War, according to Heraclitus, is "the father of all things." Man always wages war. He is a warring being. This is his ontological root. He wages war for the truth, for love, for right, for good. Sometimes war drives him too far, and he lets his hands down. But he never lets off, and he begins anew. As long as a man lives, he wages war.

During the span of our entire history, we Russians always waged wars. As a rule, when we did not wage war we decayed. Why, in fact, must we stop waging war, if enemies live around us, who encroach on our space, on our *narod*, on our religion? If they were not encroaching, it would be a different matter, but then they would not be humans.

Uninterrupted war with sin goes to the heart of man. The worst outcome here would be pacifism, the reconciliation of grace and sin. This would be neither a reconciliation nor a compromise, but the victory of sin. The Terrestrial Church in the Orthodox tradition is called the Militant Church. In the body of conservative philosophy, the topic of war must be raised transparently, calmly, without malicious joy or sadism, responsibly. But we must know and think of ourselves as warriors, as a warring *narod*, a warring country, a warring Church.

The Tripartite Structure of the Conservative Episteme

If we consider the above-mentioned trichotomous structure, we will uncover three pivotal disciplines among all scientific disciplines. The highest of them is theology, because religion is not only worship and ritual, but also the deepest worldview system. It is the science of spirit.

Theology must be the crown of education. Without it, the entire conservative episteme will be incomplete and will hang in the air. Theology is the royal science, the science of sciences, not simply one of the humanities and sociological sciences, but the most important among them. All other sciences are a road to theology.

On the second level one should put ethnosociology. Among us, almost nothing at all was said in science, down to the present day, of either the *narod* or the *ethnos*. That is not surprising: for communists, the subject of history is the class; for liberals, it is the individual. In neither case is room left for the *narod* or the *ethnos*. Ethnosociology is the fundamental science of Empire and the conservative project. If we do not correctly define beforehand our *narod* and that of other peoples, with whom we find ourselves in interaction, we will simply be incompetent to speak about conservatism. Ethnosociology is not only the definition of the formal ethnological characteristics of a *narod*, but a study of that which is constitutive for the *ethnos*, an understanding of its ontology, its being.

And finally, the third discipline is the science of territorial space, geopolitics. Here everything is obvious, since geopolitics is by definition a science, studying the relation of a state to a territorial space. Occupying the last place in the hierarchy of the pivotal disciplines of the conservative episteme, it has enormous applied significance.

In this way, theology, ethnosociology and geopolitics constitute the trichotomous structure of science in the conservative understanding. The teaching of other social and humanitarian sciences must line up around these three pivots, agree with them, and orient themselves around their force-lines. In special cases, sociologists and geopoliticians can study economics and jurisprudence. They are undoubtedly important, but not for conservatives. Let liberals and communists start with economics and ignore all the rest; such is their philosophy. Conservatives must act differently, in accordance with their philosophical positions. Today we find ourselves under hypnosis, thinking that "economics is serious," while theology, on the other hand, is "optional" (if not unscientific). But in fact, everything is strictly the other way around. He who knows eternity knows everything. He who knows the temporary material regularities of the circulation of money, merchants and goods, does not even know that which he supposes himself to know.

Economics is secondary, derivative from philosophy. The roots of economic theory lie precisely in philosophy, not in economics. Thus, Adam Smith, the founder of bourgeois political economy, was convinced that he was simply developing certain philosophical positions of his teacher John Locke with regard to the sphere of the economy. Marxism is the development of the philosophy of Hegel with an accent on economic laws and a specific philosophy of history, defined from the position of the oppressed classes, and, in the first place, the proletariat.

The implementation of the conservative episteme is the necessary condition for the working out of a full-fledged conservative project. This stage cannot be passed over.

PART II
EMPIRE AND THE EURASIAN IDEA

CHAPTER 3

The West and its Challenge

What Do We Understand By "The West"?

The term "the West" can be construed in different ways. Thus, we should first of all clarify what we mean by that term and examine how the concept has evolved historically.

It is perfectly evident that "the West" is not a purely geographical term. The sphericity of the Earth makes such a definition simply incorrect: what is for one point the West is for another the East. But nobody includes this sense in the concept of "the West." On closer examination, however, we discover an important fact: the concept of "the West" takes by default as its zero-line, from which its coordinates are set, precisely Europe. And it is not by accident that the zero-line meridian passes through Greenwich, in accord with an international convention. Eurocentrism is built in to this very procedure.

Although many ancient states (Babylon, China, Israel, Russia, Japan, Iran, Egypt, etc.) thought of themselves as "the center of the world," "middle empires," "celestial," "kingdoms under the sun," and so on, in international practice, Europe became the central coordinate. More narrowly, Western Europe did. It is customary to set a vector in the direction of the East and a vector in the direction of the West starting from precisely there. Thus, even in the narrow geographical sense we see the world from a Eurocentric point of view, and "the West" at the same time presents itself as the center, "the middle."

Europe and Modernity

In a historical sense, Europe became the place where the transition from traditional to modern society occurred. What is more, this transition was accomplished through the development of tendencies autochthonic to European culture and European civilization. Developing in a specific direction principles contained in Greek philosophy and Roman law, through the interpretation of Christian teaching — at first in the Catholic-Scholastic, and later in the Protestant spirit — Europe came to create a model of society unique among other civilizations and cultures. In the first place, this society:

- was built on secular (atheistic) bases;
- proclaimed the idea of social and technical progress;
- created the foundations of the contemporary scientific view of the world;
- developed and introduced a model of political democracy;
- regarded capitalistic (market) relations as of paramount importance;
- transitioned from an agrarian to an industrial economy.

In short, Europe became the territorial space of the contemporary world.

Because within the borders of Europe itself the more *avant-garde* areas of development of the paradigm of modernity were such countries as England, Holland and France, located west of Central (and especially Eastern) Europe, the concepts "Europe" and "the West" gradually became synonyms: the properly speaking "European" culture, as different from other cultures, consisted precisely in the transition from traditional society to the society of modernity, while this, in turn, occurred first of all in the European West.

Thus, from the 17th to the 18th centuries the term "the West" acquired a precise civilizational sense, becoming a synonym of "Modernity," "modernization," and "progress," social, industrial, economic and technological development. From now on, all that was involved in the processes of modernization was automatically attached to the West. "Modernization" and "Westernization" proved to be synonymous.

The Idea of "Progress" as the Basis for Political Colonization and Cultural Racism

The identity of "modernization" and "Westernization" requires some clarifications, which will lead us to very important practical conclusions. The issue is that the formation in Europe of the unprecedented civilization of the modern era led to a particular cultural arrangement, which at first formed the self-consciousness of the Europeans themselves and later also of all those who found themselves under their influence. The sincere conviction grew that the path of development of Western culture, and especially the transition from traditional society to contemporary society, was not only a peculiarity of Europe and the peoples that populate it, but a universal law of development, obligatory for all other countries and peoples. Europeans, "people of the West," were the first to pass through this decisive phase, but all others are thought fatally doomed to go along the same path, because this is the supposedly "objective" logic of world history. "Progress" demands it.

The idea arose that the West is the obligatory model of the historical development of all mankind, and world history — as in the past, so in the present and future — was and is conceived of as a repetition of those stages that the West, in its development, already passed through or is presently approaching, in advance of all others. In all places where Europeans encountered "non-Western" cultures, which preserved "traditional society" and its way, Europeans made an unequivocal diagnosis: "barbarism," "savagery," "backwardness," "absence of civilization," "sub-normality." Thus, gradually the West became the idea of a normative criterion for the evaluation of the peoples and cultures of the entire world. The further they were from the West (in its newest historical phase), the more "defective" and "inferior" they were thought to be.

The Archaic Roots of Western Exclusiveness

It is interesting to analyze the origin of this universalist arrangement, in which the stages of the West's development are equated with the generally obligatory logic of world history.

The deepest and most archaic roots can be found in the cultures of ancient tribes. It is characteristic of ancient societies to identify the concept "human" with the concept "belonging to the tribe" or *ethnos*, which leads at times to their denying the member of another tribe the status of "human," or placing him on an inferior level. By this logic, tribesmen from other tribes or enslaved peoples became the class of serfs, excluded from human society and deprived of all kinds of rights and privileges. This model — fellow tribesmen = people, foreign tribesmen = not people — lies at the foundation of the social, legal, and political institutions of the past, as was analyzed in detail by Hegel (in particular, by the Hegelian Kojeve) through the pair of figures, Master-Slave. The Master was everything, the Slave, nothing. The status of human belonged to the Master as a privilege. The Slave was equated, even legally, to domesticated livestock or to an object of production.

This model of domination proved much more stable than one could have imagined. It moved on in modified form into the modern era. Thus arose the complex of ideas that paradoxically combined democracy and freedom within European societies themselves with rigid racist arrangements and cynical colonization in their relations with other, "less developed" peoples.

It is significant that after more than a thousand year gap the institution of slavery, what's more, on racial grounds, returned in Western societies — in the first place in the USA, but also in the countries of Latin America — precisely in the modern era, in the era of the spread of democratic and liberal ideas. Moreover, the theory of "progress" serves, in fact, as a basis for the inhuman exploitation by Europeans and white Americans of aboriginals: Native Indians and African slaves.

It increasingly appears that by the formation of the civilization of the modern era in Europe, the model of the Master-Slave was transferred from Europe itself to the rest of the world in the form of colonial policies.

Empire and its Influence on Contemporary Westernization

Another important source for this influence was the idea of Empire. Europeans explicitly rejected that idea at the dawn of the modern era, but it penetrated into the unconscious of Western man. Empire — both Roman and Christian (the Byzantine in the East and the Holy Roman Empire of German nations in the West) — was thought of as the Universe, the inhabitants of which are people (citizens), while those beyond it are "subhumans," "barbarians," "heretics," "gentiles," or even fantastic creatures: man-eaters, monsters, vampires, "Gog and Magog," and so on. Here the tribal division between one's own (people) and strangers (non-people) is carried over to a higher and more abstract plane: citizens of empire (participants in the Universe) and non-citizens (inhabitants of the global periphery).[1]

This stage of generalizing who is and is not to be counted a person can be looked at entirely as a transitional stage between the archaic and the contemporary West. After formally rejecting Empire and its

---

1 Already in the 17th century European and American authors (in particular, Jesuits) posed the question of whether Native Indians belong to the native population of America, to human kind, or whether they are some sort of animal.

religious foundations, contemporary Europe preserved imperialism by transferring it to the level of values and interests. Progress and technological development were henceforth thought of as a European mission, in the name of which a planetary colonization strategy was implemented.

Thus, having broken away formally from traditional society, the modern era transferred some basic arrangements of traditional society (the archaic division into the pair person/non-person on ethnic grounds, the model of the Slave-Master, the imperialist identification of its civilization with the Universe and of all others with "savages," and so on) to the new conditions of life. As an idea and planetary strategy, the West became an ambitious project for the new establishment of a world government, this time dedicated to the "enlightenment," "development," and "progress" of all humanity. This is a kind of "humanitarian imperialism."

It is important to note that the thesis about progress was not a simple cover for the egoistic predatory interests of Western people in their colonial expansion. Faith in the universalism of Western values and in the logic of historical development was entirely sincere. Interests and values coincided in this case. This gave tremendous energy to the trailblazers, sailors, travellers, and businessman of the West to settle the planet. They not only sought profits, but also carried enlightenment to the "savages."

Cruel robbery, cynical exploitation, and a new wave of slave holding, together with the modernization and the technological development of colonial territories, together formed the basis of the West as an idea and global practice.

Modernization: Endogenous and Exogenous

Here we should make one important observation. Starting from the 16th century, the process of planetary modernization began to unfold from the territory of Western Europe. It strictly coincided with the colonization by the West of new lands, where, as a rule, peoples preserving the foundations of traditional society lived. But gradually modernization affected everyone: both Westerners and non-Westerners. Somehow or other, everyone is modernized. But the essence of this process remains different in different cases.

In the West itself—first of all in England, France, Holland, and especially the USA, a country built as a laboratory experiment in modernity on supposedly "empty land" — modernization is distinguished by its endogenous character. It grows from the consistent development of cultural, social, religious, and political processes contained in the very foundations of European society. This does not come about everywhere simultaneously and with one and the same intensity. Such peoples as the Germans, Spaniards, and Italians, with whom modernization proceeds in a somewhat slower rhythm than it does with their European neighbors from the West, lagged behind. Still, the modern era for European peoples ensues from within and in accordance with the natural logic of their development. The modernization of the countries and peoples of Europe emerges according to internal laws. Developing from objective preconditions and corresponding to the will and mood of the majority of European people, it is endogenous. That is, it has an internal principle.

It is a completely different matter with those countries and peoples that are pulled into the process of modernization despite their will, becoming victims of colonization or else being reluctant to oppose European expansion. Of course, conquering countries and peoples or sending black slaves to the USA, the people of the West furthered the process of modernization. Together with the colonial administration, they brought out new orders and foundations, and also the technique and logic of economic processes, mores, social-political structures, and legal institutions. Black slaves, especially after the victory of the abolitionist North, became members of a more developed society (although they also remained second-class people) than the archaic tribes of Africa from which slave traders had taken them. The modernization of colonies and enslaved nations cannot be denied. Even in this case, the West proves to be the motor of modernization. But here the process can be called exogenous, occurring from without, imposed, brought in.

Non-Western peoples and cultures remain in the conditions of traditional society, developing in accord with their own cycles and their own inner logic. In them there are also periods of ascent and decline, religious reforms and internal discord, economic catastrophes and technical discoveries. But these rhythms correspond to a different, non-Western model of development, follow a different logic, are directed to different goals, and decide different problems.

The main feature of exogenous modernization is that it does not emerge from the internal needs and natural development of traditional society, which, when left to itself, probably would never have come to those structures and models that were put together in the West. In other words, such modernization is coerced and imposed from without.

Consequently, the synonymous series modernization = Westernization can be continued: it is also colonization (the introduction of external authority). The oppressed majority of mankind, excluding Europeans and the direct descendants of American colonists, were subjected to precisely this violent, coerced, external modernization. It impacted the traumatic and internal inconsistencies of the majority of contemporary societies of Asia, the East, and the Third World. This is sick Modernity, the West as caricature.

Two Types of Society with Exogenous Modernization

Now, in all societies exposed to exogenous modernization, we can distinguish two big classes:

- Those that preserved political-economic independence (or strove for it in anti-colonial wars);
- Those that lost political-economic independence.

In the second case, we are dealing with a pure colony, one that has completely lost its independence and no more participates in the values of modernity than Indians on North American reservations. Such societies can be archaic (like some African, South American or Pacific tribes), but they partially intersect with the higher technological and rather modernized structures unfolded on that same territorial space by the colonizers. Here there is almost no semantic intersection between the indigenous people and the modernizers: the status of local societies barely differs from the status of inhabitants of zoological gardens, or in the best case of a conservation area populated by endangered species. In this case, modernization does not concern the local population, which continues not to notice it and only encounters technical restrictions, in the guise of barbed wire and iron lattice cells.

When we are dealing with a society that has obligatorily traversed a specific path along the lines of Westernization and exogenous modernization, but has done this in response to the threat of colonization from Europe (the West) and managed to preserve its independence, the process of modernization (= Westernization) acquires a more complicated character. One can call this: "defensive modernization."

Here the center of attention is the balance between the values peculiar to the traditional society, preserved for the support of identity, and those models and systems necessary to import from the West for the creation of the prerequisites and conditions for partial (defensive) modernization. At the same time, subjectivity is preserved in these societies, which determine their own interests, making them keen to oppose the colonial initiatives of the West.

Thus, the following picture emerges. In order to defend its interests before the face of Western onslaught, a country (society) is compelled to adopt certain values from that very same West, but to combine them with their original values. Huntington called this phenomenon "modernization without Westernization."

Incidentally, this concept carries in itself a few contradictions. Inasmuch as modernization and Westernization are essentially synonymous (The West = Modernity), it is impossible to modernize in separation from the West and without copying its values. In traditional societies outside the natural habitat of European culture, preconditions for modernization are simply absent. That is why we are not talking about a complete rejection of "Westernization," but of a balance between one's values and those imposed from the West that would satisfy the conditions for the preservation of identity (difference from the West — specifically, on the level of principle!) and the development of defensive technologies able to compete with the West in basic vital regions (which is impossible to accomplish without being included in the "Western" context.) Thus, there are a variety of exogenous modernizations, based on the presence of independent interests (principally different from those of the colonizing intentions of the West) and on the combination of one's own interests with the pragmatically imported values of the West. (We can say that this is "modernization + partial Westernization.")

Some examples of exogenous modernization are Russia (throughout the entire course of modernity, which by itself affords a sufficiently unique case!), contemporary China, India, Brazil, Japan, some Islamic countries, and the countries of the Pacific region (which entered into this process much later, in the last century). Besides Russia, the other countries travelling down this road were at certain times colonies of the West and received independence relatively recently. Otherwise, like Japan, they suffered defeat in war and were occupied.

In any case, this type of exogenous modernization brings to the forefront the question of the balance of one's own interests and foreign interests, or the problem of the proportion and quality of elements belonging to two cultural-historical and civilizational forms, the local, conservative foundations of traditional society and the so-called "universal" and "progressive" models of Western civilization.

This proportion is the most important thing and constitutes the essence of the relations between Russia and the West.

We shall return to this a little later, but will first make a few geopolitical observations.

The Conception of "West" and "East" in the Yalta World

Now let us consider the geopolitical aspects of the problems we have been discussing and the transformation of the concept of "the West" in the 20th century, which is related to them.

After the end of the Second World War the concept of "the West" started to be applied geopolitically to the totality of developed countries that had set out on the capitalistic path of development. This was one correction of the concept. Such a "West" is practically identical with capitalism and liberal-democratic ideology. Those countries that moved forward along this path further than the others were in fact thought of as "the West" in the construction of a bipolar world, called also the Yalta world (from the location of the conference of the heads of the counties in the anti-Hitler coalition that foreordained the map of the world in the second half of the 20th century: Stalin, Roosevelt and Churchill).

This time the concept of "the West" differs partially from the one we provided earlier. First, even the communist regimes belonged ideologically to "the West" in the broad sense — in the first place the USSR — insofar as they adopted "Western European" theories of socialism and communism (which were built on observations concerning the history of the political-economic developments of precisely Western societies, together with a corresponding faith in progress and the universalism of these regularities for all humanity).

Meanwhile, Marxism became the favorite model for the modernization of traditional societies; it could combine the preservations of their own geopolitical interests and the partial preservation of local traditional values with the powerful, imported apparatus of modernizing and peculiarly Western ideas, structures, interests, and theories. Thus, Marxism — Soviet, Chinese (Maoism), Vietnamese, North Korean, and so on — should be examined as a variant of exogenous modernization. Moreover, from the point of view of technological and ideological competition, this project proved relatively successful.

Although dogmatic Marxism pretended that it would replace capitalism once capitalism had reached the critical stage in its implementation, in practice everything happened entirely differently. Communist parties won in those societies where capitalism was in rudimentary condition, while traditional society (agrarian, in the first place) prevailed both in the economic and cultural sense. In other words, the actualized, victorious Marxism was the refutation of the theory of its ideological founder. On the other hand, the history of capitalist societies shows that Marx's predictions of the inevitability of proletarian revolution in them have been disproved by time. Marx insisted that the proletarian revolution could not occur in Russia (and in other countries with a predominance of "the Asian mode of production"), but that is just where it happened. In societies with developed capitalism, nothing similar happened.

From this only one conclusion suggests itself: in communist regimes, Marxism was not what it proclaimed to be, but was rather a model of exogenous modernization in which Western values were adopted only partially and were tacitly combined with local religious-eschatological and messianic tendencies. On the whole, this procedure of specific modernization — alter-modernization along the socialistic (totalitarian), but not capitalistic (democratic) path — served for the defense of the geopolitical and strategic interests of independent states, which were striving to repel the colonial attacks of Europe and (later) America.

After the Second World War, the strategic block that formed around the USSR, the avant-garde of this alter-modernization was called "the East." Although at issue was really a variant of exogenous modernization, formally the Marxist system of values was based on the paradigm of modernity in just such a degree as were capitalist societies. Sometimes, in the political science of the Yalta period, instead of the formula "the East" ("the communist East," "the Eastern Bloc,") the expression "the Second World" was used. It is more precise and embraces those countries that took in accelerated industrialization with partial and rather specific modernization (of the communist kind) and, most importantly, managed to preserve geopolitical independence, having avoided (or freed themselves from) direct colonization.

In this case, the concept "Third World" acquires significance.

"The First World," that is, "the West" in the terminology of the post-War period, comprises countries with endogenous modernization (Europe, America), and also the one case of exogenous, but extremely successful technological modernization in the guise of the occupation of Japan, which directed the internal energies of a conquered nation to massive economic growth by Western standards. But at the same time Japan lost its geopolitical independence and in the strategic sense became a resigned and fractured US colony.

"The Second World" signifies the countries of exogenous modernization that managed to avail themselves of the totalitarian-socialist methods of modernization, with the partial and relatively successful borrowing of Western technology and the preservation of independence from the capitalist West. This, in the understanding of the Yalta-based world, was called "the East."

And finally, "the Third World" referred to countries of exogenous modernization that dropped behind the development of both the "First" and of the "Second" world, did not possess complete sovereignty, preserved the foundations of traditional society and were forced to rely on either "the West" or "the East," thus being colonies, subordinate to the one or the other.

And so, if we limit our considerations to the conditions of "the Cold War" (the bipolar world), the concept of "the West" emerges as synonymous with the capitalist camp, "the First World," including the more developed and richer countries of North America, Europe, and Japan.

The intellectual headquarters of the integration of "the First World," "the West" in this concrete sense, was the Trilateral Commission, created on the basis of the American Council on Foreign Relations and composed of representatives of the elites of the USA, Europe, and Japan. Thus, starting from the 1960s a specific segment of intellectuals, bankers, politicians, and scholars of "the West," took on itself historical responsibility for the process of globalization and the creation of a "world government" on the basis of the final victory of "the West" over the rest of the world, in the geopolitical, moral, economic, and ideological senses.

In the 1990s "the West" Becomes Globalization

Still another transformation of the concept of "the West" was put to the test in the 1990s, when the architecture of the bipolar (Yalta-based) world collapsed. From then on, the liberal-capitalist model became the most important and the only one. Communism as a project of alter-modernization came to a crash, notwithstanding the competition, and the military-political and economic might of the USA irrefutably surpassed that of all other countries. The one-sided capitulation of the USSR and the Warsaw Bloc in "the Cold War" with the ensuing dissolution opened the path of globalization and the construction of a unipolar world. The American philosopher, neoconservative Francis Fukuyama, started speaking of "the end of history," of "the replacement of politics by economics," and "the transformation of the planet into a unified and homogenous market."

This meant that the concept "the West" transformed into a global concept without opposition, inasmuch as nothing more contended against not only the very idea of modernization, but also its more orthodox and historically "Western" liberal-capitalist project. So successful and weighty a victory of "the West" over "the East" — that is, of "the First World" over "the Second" — essentially liquidated the alternatives to modernization and made it the one and only uncontested substance of world history. Everyone who wanted to stay "contemporary" had to recognize this unconditional preeminence of "the West," to express loyalty to it, and also once and for all to repudiate all their own interests — even if they differed in some aspects or were contrary to the interests of the USA (or NATO more broadly) — and become flag-bearers for the unipolar world.

Henceforth, the problem was put only in this way: into which segment of the global "West" will one or another country, one or another state, be integrated? If modernization and, correspondingly, Westernization were introduced successfully, then the opportunity appeared of integrating with "the golden billion" or the zone of "the Rich North." If for some reason this did not work out, there remained the possibility of integration into the belt of the world periphery, into the zone of "the Poor South." Meanwhile, the planetary division of labor offered the promise of modernization to even "the Poor South," but this time in accordance with the colonial scenario, when political slavery was replaced with economic slavery, while the import of Western cultural standards methodically eradicated indigenous values (thus, the residents of South Korea, having received a vigorous impulse of exogenous modernization of the colonial type together with volatile economic growth, faced an almost total dissemination of Protestantism amidst traditional, shamanistic, Buddhist and Confucian society). To plug into the Global West did not guarantee anything, but it gave these countries a chance.

There were similar reforms in Russia, too, which appeared as a new political formation after the fall of the USSR, which itself had inherited the Russian Empire geopolitically. Russia also tried to integrate with the global West, counting on a place in "the Rich North" and hoping to "make communion" to modernization in its main (capitalist), not roundabout (socialist) path. Meanwhile, Russia, like all other countries, was given the offer at first to reject global pretensions, and later even local ones, delighting in the role of strategic satellite of the USA among still less modernized nations, without any special privileges whatever. Essentially, external controls were brought into the country.

The ruling powers accommodated the colonial elite, reformers-Westernizers, and oligarchs, which thought of themselves as managers working for the global transnational corporations with headquarters on the other side of the Atlantic.

Globalization

At the beginning of the 1990s, when "the end of history" seemed not only close at hand, but actually accomplished, the concept of "the West" almost overlapped with the concept "world," which was nailed down in the term "globalization."

Globalization represents the last point in the practical realization of the foundational pretensions of "the West" to the universality of its historical experience and its system of values.

Penetrating into various societies and cultures and combining humanitarian projects with colonial methods of satisfying their own interests (in the first place in the sphere of natural resources), the process of globalization made "the West" a global concept. By leaps and bounds, the world moved to a unipolar model, where the developed center (USA the nucleus, trans-Atlantic society) concerned itself with the underdeveloped periphery.[2]

At length, a model was built up, described in Huntington's classic *Clash of Civilizations*: "the West and the rest." But in the model of globalization, these "rest" are looked at in no way other than in relation to "the West"; this is also "the West," only underdeveloped and imperfect — a kind of "semi-West."

And here already in new historical conditions and across a line of transformations and semantic alterations we again come up against the cultural racism and liberal-democratic secular "messianism" that we discovered among the sources of the epoch of Modernity and in the initial definition of the concept of "the West."

Post-Modernity and "the West"

Another interesting process occurred in the 1990s regarding the content of the concept "modernization." Modernization, which was carried out at various speeds and with various characteristics in one way or another in the whole world from the start of the Modern Era in Western Europe, approached its own logical completion at the end of the 20th century. What's more, this naturally happened in the West itself: the one who started first and proceeded according to natural principles to the modernization of traditional society reached the finish line first. Thus, overcoming both the inertial resistance of conservative structures and, at a specific time and very effectively, competition from socialist alter-modernization, Modernity in its liberal-capitalist form reached its determinate limits and the end of the implementation of its program. The direct opposition of alternative ideologies was broken, while to overcome the global periphery's passive resistance became a technical matter. Where there was still resistance, it could be regarded as the "inertial reaction of objective surroundings," but not as a com-

---

[2] Thomas Barnett. *The Pentagon's New Map: War and Peace in the Twenty-First Century* (New York: Putnam, 2004).

petitive strategy. The battle against traditional society and its attempts to be presented in a new guise (alter-modernization, socialism) ended with the victory of liberalism. And in the West itself, modernization reached its internal limits, having reached the lowest point of Western culture.

This condition of the final exhaustion of the agenda for the process of modernization generated a rather specific phenomenon in the West: postmodernity.

The gist of postmodernity consists in the fact that the end of the modernization of traditional societies carries the people of the West into principally new conditions. One can liken this long process to the accomplishment of an intended purpose. People seated on a train, travelling to an incredibly distant station, become so used to the movement, which does not cease for a few generations, that they cannot imagine life differently. They see existence as development directed toward a distant reference point, about which all remember and toward which all strive, but which all the time remains very remote. And suddenly the train arrives at the final station. Platform, station-house... the goal has been reached, the problems, decided...but people have become so accustomed to moving all the time that they cannot come into themselves after the shock of colliding with their realized dream. When the goal is reached, there is nowhere else to strive to, nowhere to go, nothing to move toward. Progress reached its maximum point. Precisely this is "the end of history," or "post-history" (Gelen, Vattimo, Baudrillard).

With this metaphor, one can completely describe the condition of postmodernity. Here, there is the feeling of both success and disappointment. In any case, this is no longer modernity, nor the Enlightenment, nor the Modern Era. The critical faction of postmodern philosophers subjected to derision various stages of the movement to this goal and began to speak ironically of the illusions and hopes with which those who started the movement comforted themselves, not suspecting of what kind the realization of that goal would be. Others offered to break with the critical feeling and perceive "the brave new world" as it is, without going into details and doubts.

In any case, whether estimated positively or negatively, postmodernity represented a terminal state. Faith in progress finished its business and ceded its place to playful temporality.[3] Reality, having earlier displaced myth, religion, and the sacred, itself transformed into virtuality. Man, at the dawn of the Modern Era, after overthrowing God from the pedestal, is himself henceforth prepared to yield the king's place to a post-human breed, to cyborgs, mutants, clones, and to all the products of "liberated technique."

The Post-West

In the era of globalization, the West not only becomes global and omnipresent itself (as expressed in the uniformity of world fashions, the general diffusion of computer and information technologies, the ubiquitous establishment of the market economy and liberal-democratic political and legal systems), but in its nucleus, in the center of a unipolar world, it also qualitatively changes the "Rich North" from modernity to postmodernity.

Henceforth for the first time in history the appeal to this nuclear West — the West in its highest manifestation – does not carry modernity behind it (of whatever kind, exogenous or endogenous), as the West itself is henceforth synonymous not with modernity but with postmodernity. But postmodernity, with its ironies, pure technologicity, recycling of the old, and spent faith in progress, no longer offers

---

[3] Gilles Deleuze. *The Logic of Sense* (New York: Columbia University Press, 1993). Deleuze's concept of "the zone" (rational temporality, having the past and the future, but not having the existential present) and "chronos" (existential temporality, representing the pure, present, linear sense — that is, of the future and the past); both temporalities, according to Deleuze, acquire freedom in the condition of the "rhizome." Cf. also: Alexander Dugin, *Post-philosophy* (Moscow, 2009).

its periphery even the distant prospect of development. "The end of history," which came, raises absolutely different questions, before the weight and significance of which the pulling up by "the West" to its own level of "the Poor South" looks like an absolutely unnecessary, purposeless, and senseless task: if anything can be found there, the answers to the new problems of the postmodern epoch surely will not be one of those things.

Thus, those who relate by inertia to the rooted West in the search for modernization in new conditions are doomed to a colossal disappointment: having traversed the entire path of modernization to its end, the West has no more stimulus either to move in this direction itself or to entice others behind it. The West has moved on to a qualitatively new stage. Now it is no longer the West, but the Post-West, the peculiar, deeply modified West of postmodernity.

Technically and technologically it dominates completely, and the processes of globalization develop at full speed. But this is no longer a progressive development. It is a circular movement around an even more problematic center. The architecture of postmodernity makes constructions where styles and epochs are fancifully intermixed, while in the place of the central point of the architectural ensemble gapes a hole. This is the absent center, the pole of the circle, representing the downfall into non-being.

Such, too, is the substantial structure of the unipolar world. In the center of the global West — in the USA and the countries of the transatlantic alliance — there blazes the black, senseless hole of postmodernity realized.

The Gap Between the Theory and Practice of Globalism

The last metamorphosis of the West during its transformation to postmodernity, which we described above, is a purely theoretical construction. This picture was put together at the start of the 1990s. The logic of world history was conceptualized by Western thinkers who have not yet ceded the road to post-humanity (possibly to thinking automatons). But between this theoretical conception and its embodiment there remained a decisive gap. Reflection on the nature and structure of postmodernity and the West led even its own ardent apologists to a state of horror and despair. For instance, at a certain moment Francis Fukuyama moved away from the ideological picture that he himself drew at the start of the 1990s and offered to give it back, preserving the West in the condition in which it found itself before it had arrived at its final station.[4] Fukuyama's critics, Huntington included, also overstated the quality and quantity of the barriers to be overcome by the West in order for it to become truly global and ubiquitous. From different points of view, everyone started to cling to the remnants of modernity, with its nation states, faith in progress, moralizations, mentorship, and phobias, to which everyone has long ago become accustomed. Then a decision was made to prolong the movement to the intended goal, or at least to simulate the rocking of the wagons and the banging of tires on the joints of the rails.

Today the West dwells precisely in this gap between that which it theoretically must become in the era of globalism and by the fact that it overcame all obstacles and defeated all alternatives, and that which it utterly does not want to recognize as the new global architecture of postmodernity, with a hole rather than a center. However, in this gap, infinitely small and constantly contracting, there occur very important processes, which constantly change the general world picture.

All of this actively exerts an influence on Russia.

---

4   Francis Fukuyama. *Our Post-Human Future: Consequences of the Biotechnology Revolution* (New York: Farrar Straus & Giroux, 2002).

USA and the EU: The Two Poles of the Western World at the Start of the 21st Century

The fluctuation of the West in the gap between completed modernity and incipient postmodernity is also reflected in the geopolitical sphere. Thus, the disappearance of a global competitor, in the guise of the USSR (the alter-modernization project), called transatlantic civilization into question. The lack of an enemy in the East made the connection of the USA and Europe in the framework of "the nuclear West" not quite so obvious and self-evident. It became apparent that the transatlantic West was split into the USA and the European Union.

The center of the West during the 20th century constantly shifted to the other side of the Atlantic, to the USA. After the Second World War, the United States took upon itself the mission of being the avant-garde of the West. It became a superpower, providing by its might the military-strategic safety and economic prosperity of European countries.

After the fall of the USSR, the role of the center of the West became even more firmly established in the USA. This coincided with European integration and the creation in Europe in essence of a supranational government, a government of the postmodern kind.[5] Once a cradle of the West as a phenomenon, Europe in turn became "the East" in relation to the USA. The United States traversed the path of modernization and post-modernization further than Europe, and the Old World, in comparison to the New, transformed into something independent.

Thus a geopolitical picture was formed, where in the space of the West itself there arose a determinate dualism. On one hand, the USA became the most "advanced" West. But Europe, on the other hand, attempted to discover its own separate, particular path.

---

5 Robert Cooper. *The Breaking of Nations: Order and Chaos in the Twenty-First Century* (New York: Grove Press, 2003).

There were even philosophical arguments about the differences between Europe and the US. Some American neo-conservatives (in particular, Robert Kagan)[6] proposed to look at American civilization as ensuing from the conception of the menacing state of Hobbes' *Leviathan* and the European Union as the embodiment of the pacifist ideas of Kant, with his civil society, tolerance, and human rights. Other classifications were offered too. In any case, the US and Europe started to reinterpret their identities, their values, and their relation to modernity and postmodernity.

This was even more evident on the level of interests. The European Union, as the first commercial and second economic power in the world, recognized that its interests in Arab countries, and also in relation to Russian and other countries of the East, regularly differ from American interests and often conflict with them. This became especially clear at the time of the Iraq war, when NATO command did not support the American invasion, while the leaders of France and Germany (Chirac and Schroeder), together with Putin, protested sharply against the war.

We can describe the situation like this: the USA and Europe today have common values, but different interests. The difference of interests, and the recognition of this difference, is particularly noticeable in such continental European countries as France, Germany, Italy, and Spain and in the continentalist tendency towards the representation of Europe as a self-reliant geopolitical player, which as far as possible must become independent of the USA. In the most extreme cases, continentalists affirm that the USA and Europe have not only different interests but also different values (see, for instance, the French philosopher Alain de Benoist).[7]

---

6   Robert Kagan. *Of Paradise and Power* (New York: Vintage Books, 2004).
7   Alain de Benoist. *L'Europe, Tiers-monde, Meme Combat* (Paris, 1992).

On the other pole of Europe are found those who underline in every way possible the unity of values and on this basis insist on the accommodation of European interests to American ones. To this pole relate Euro-Atlanticists (England, the countries of Eastern Europe — Poland, Hungary, Romania, the Czech Republic, the Baltic states, and so on).

Two different tendencies in Europe itself create a dual identity. On one hand, we are concerned with continental Europe, on the other, with Atlantic (pro-American) Europe. Both sides relate to the concept of "the West" in different ways: the continentals think that if Europe is "the West," then the USA is something different. The Atlanticists, on the contrary, strive in many ways to identify the fate of Europe and America as a unified civilization, where the Atlantic is a kind of "inner lake" (just as the Greek and Roman ecumenes thought about the Mediterranean Sea in their time). For Euro-Atlanticists, the European Union and the USA together represent "the West," and the USA is its *avant-garde*.

The Identity of Russia: Country or...?

Now we move to a consideration of the identity of contemporary Russia. The preliminary examination of what we ought to understand by "the West" supplied us with secure instruments that allow us to determine what we understand by "Russia." Now, we can wholly concretely and soundly describe the correlation of both one and the other in the present and the probable future.

There are two principally different conceptions of contemporary Russia (by the way, this could be said also of the Romanov reign, where lively discussions were held apropos the same question).

One can understand Russia either as a country or as an independent civilization. The structure of our relation to the West will depend on the decision we make about how we understand Russia.

If Russia is a country, it should be grouped together with other countries, for instance with such countries as France, Germany, England, or the USA. Consequently, it will have to be appropriated to Europe (according to its partial geographic arrangement, the predominance of Christianity, and the Indo-European origins of the dominant Slavic *ethnoses* — in the first place, of Great Russians) and accordingly to "the West." Many consider Russia a European state. This opinion prevails among:

- the Romanov aristocracy;
- Russian Westernizers;
- the contemporary Russian political elite.

From the mouths of Putin and Medvedev, we repeatedly heard it said that, "Russia is a European country."

If we take this position, we must almost immediately admit that Russia is "a bad, an entirely horrible European country," inasmuch as it clearly falls outside of what is commonly considered the normative way of Western civilization. The moral, social, political, cultural, and psychological identity of Russia differs so much from that of European and American society that a doubt at once arises concerning its belonging to the West.

The most important criterion here is the nature of Russian modernization. When we consider it, we clearly see all the signs of exogeneity, that is, the external occurrence of the modernizing impulse, which did not ripen inside of the society itself, but was grafted on artfully and forcefully (in an authoritarian or totalitarian manner) from above by the tyrannical power of a despot (Peter the Great) or by extremist fanatics (the Bolsheviks). Russia lacked and lacks:

- capitalism,
- individualism,
- democracy,
- rationalism,

- personal responsibility,
- legal self-consciousness,
- civil society.

On the contrary, there grew and are still growing today the arrangements of traditional society:

- paternalism,
- collectivism,
- hierarchy,
- a relation to the state and to society as family,
- the superiority of morality over rights, ethical reasoning over rational, and so on.

Moreover, Russia absorbed many European characteristics, both moral and technological, but it adapted them to its own, particular way of life and forced them to work in the service of its own interests and values. Russia actively adopted different elements from the West, but persistently did not become the West. Hence the extreme irritation of the people of the West (and especially of Russian Westernizers) regarding Russia, which they represent as most wicked and aggressive (a caricature of Europe), imitating the West's outward forms, but investing them with its own native Russian substance.

Russia does not only differ from European countries as they differ among themselves. When crossing the Russian border, the cultural soul itself changes. We move from one cultural-historical type to another. Russia differs from precisely Europe itself, from the West as a whole.

If we are to insist that Russia is nevertheless a part of the West and a European country, we can draw two conclusions. Either Russia must be fundamentally reformed in a Western manner (which nobody has yet been able to do, down to our day), or Russia represents a kind of other West, "a different Europe."

The first case is more commonly held. But the persistence with which the Russian nation and Russian society repudiate deep Westernization (only imitating it externally), sabotage the adoption of European values (forging them in a special nationalist mode), and scare up Western society itself with extravagant scenarios, allowing the strict imperative of Western values and arrangements to slip off or erode (which was evident both in the Tsarist and especially the Soviet period) forces us to suppose that the transformation of Russians into Europeans is an absolutely hopeless matter. And Russia will thus remain only "the not-quite West," "the second-class West," lacking the strength to absorb for real the substance of Western identity.

The second case, which holds that Russia is the West, but a different one, is no less complicated. First, even if Russians consider themselves "the West," but only a peculiar form of it — for instance, Orthodox, post-Byzantine, Slavonic, and so on — Europeans never acknowledged this and won't acknowledge it, interpreting this pretension as a "haughty and unsubstantiated ambition." Attempts to insist upon it will only increase the tension and call forth a reciprocal reaction. If Russia is the West and insists on being accepted and acknowledged as it is, the very concept of "the West," the acuteness of its historical, geopolitical, technological, and cultural vector, washes away, disperses, and is destroyed. If Russia is a part of the West, then the West is no longer the West, but rather who knows what.

And finally, both positions, which overemphasize that Russia is a European country, aggravate their contradiction by the firm recognition that Russia has its own interests, which always or almost always conflict with the interests of Western countries. The independence and freedom of the motherland was always the highest value for Russians, and this evident and persistent divergence of interests forced one to call into doubt the community of values and the sense of belonging to a common civilization. This is not the main argument, inasmuch as there were also deep contradictions between European states, but in combination with the two previous considerations, it created a favorable background for natural doubts about the hypothesis of Russia's belonging to the West.

Only the position of the extreme Westernizers is more or less consistent from a purely theoretical, abstract point of view. They affirm that Russia is a "complete monstrosity" that must be forcefully transformed into a part of the West through the eradication of all independence, the rejection of Russia's own interests, the introduction of external control, and a change in the ethno-social composition of the population. In order that Russia becomes a full-fledged European country, it must first be destroyed to its foundations. But not even the radical experiment of the Bolsheviks could cope with that task, and Russia with all its peculiarities was reborn from the ashes. For that matter, the liberal reformers and oligarchs of the 1990s also failed to accomplish the task.

However, assurance that Russia is a European country is inherent in Russia's ruling class to this day. And it is not without reason that precisely the ruling class was always the source of the modernization and Westernization of Russian society. Pushkin justly noticed that, "in Russia the government is the sole European."

Russia as a Civilization (Cultural-Historical Type)

Another view of Russia defines it as an independent civilization. This position was characteristic of the late Slavophiles (Leontiev, Danilevsky), Russian Eurasianists, the Little Russians, and National-Bolsheviks (Ustralyov, Smenovekhovtsy). In this case, Russia appears as a phenomenon that one ought to compare not with a separate European country, but with Europe as a whole, with the Islamic world, with Indian or Chinese civilization. Danilevsky called this "the cultural-historical type." One can speak of "Slavic-Orthodox" or Russian civilization. A more precise expression is "Russia-Eurasia," which was introduced in the revolution of the first Eurasianists (Trubetskoy, Savitsky, Vernadsky, Alexeev, Suvchinsky, Ilyin, and so on). This formulation underscores that one is talking not about a country or simple form of state organization, but of a civilizational unity, of a state-world.

The presence of European and Asian traits in Russia as a civilization should not lead to a hasty conclusion, as though one were speaking of the mechanical computation of things borrowed from West and East. The term "Eurasia" indicates that this is some third thing, a civilization of a special kind, comparable to both the East and West in its scale and originality, yet different from them with respect to its value-content.

If we accept the assertion that Russia is a civilization, everything stands in its right place — in the epoch of the Muscovite Kingdom, in the Saint Petersburg period, and in Soviet times. The relations of Russia and the West acquire a completed logic, and all the absurdities and paradoxes inherent in the hypothesis of "Russia as a European country" resolve themselves.

Russia-Eurasia (a distinct civilization) possesses its own original values and its own interests. The values are related to traditional society, with an accent on Orthodox faith and Russian messianism.

The imperial idea of Genghis Khan and the centralized arrangement of the Mongolian hordes proved to be the essential influence on political and social foundations. The natural development of this complex did not demand modernization and did not carry in itself the preconditions of the appearance of the ideas, principles, and tendencies that were built into the foundations of modernity in Europe. But the presence in the West of active and aggressive colonial powers, obsessively trying to promote in the East not only their interests, but also their values, compelled Russia to periodically get on the road of partial and defensive modernization (and Westernization).

This modernization was exogenous, but not colonial. Its partial or hybrid character is responsible for that caricature of Russia that roused the indignation of Russian Westernizers, starting from Chaadayev, but was also censured by the Russian Slavophiles (Khomyakov, Kirievsky, the brothers Aksakov, and so on).

In this case, Russian history appears as the cyclical pulsation of a specific civilization, returning in calm conditions to its original roots, but adopting enforced modernization (from above) in critical periods. In this light, the Petrine reforms, the "Europism" of the Romanov elite, and the Soviet experiment acquire significance and law-like regularity. Russia-Eurasia inflexibly defended its own interests and values, while sometimes forced to have recourse to Westernization-modernization for effective opposition to the West.

Russia is neither a part of the West nor a part of the East. It is a civilization in itself. And the preservation of its freedom, independence, and self-being before the face of other civilizations — both those from the West and those from the East — comprises the vector of Russian history.

Russia and the West in the 1990s

In the Soviet period, and especially during "the Cold War," Russia's civilizational mission received ideological expression in the form of Soviet society. There we find the classical combination of opposition to the West (in this case, in its liberal-capitalist bourgeoisie hypostasis) and the adoption of certain Western ideas and technologies (Marxism). This was a period of typical alter-modernization, exogenous modernization with the preservation of geopolitical independence.

Towards the end of the Soviet period, the political leadership of the USSR lost the clear understanding of foundational world processes, in large part because of the Marxists' inadequate understanding of the true role and nature of Marxism itself. Soviet pedagogues ignored the National-Bolshevistic (Eurasian) character of the USSR, and this confused them in the understanding of the deep relations between Russia and the West. Thus, in decaying post-Soviet society there arose the (suicidal) idea of turning again to the West for long-term modernization, which had stalled.

At first there was talk about the possibility of a convergence between the two systems with the preservation of mutual interests and different ways of life. But this phase quickly moved to the practice of exchanging the geopolitical position of the USSR and its allies for the economic and technological instruments of development. Once it set itself on this path, the USSR fell to the ground, and the liberal-reformers of the 1990s threw themselves before the West headlong, admitting the primacy of Western interests and values now without any conditions whatever.

The 1990s were Russia's movement to the side of the West, a desperate attempt to integrate into it on any grounds. For this reason there appeared a steady tendency of repentance for the Soviet and Tsarist past, unrestrained imitation of the liberal-democratic model in its neo-liberal form in the political and the market system, a renunciation of global and regional interests, and compliance with mainstream American policies.

However, in spite of the calculations and hopes of the reformers-Westernizers, this path, connected with the names of Yeltsin and his circle, produced no positive results.

The West did not hurry to modernize Russia for two reasons:

- Fear that Russia might return once more to the path of confrontation, reinforcing itself and establishing its power (the West understood perfectly well that Russia is no sort of European country, but rather an independent civilization and always related to her like that),
- Transitioning to postmodernity, the West itself lost its ideological interest in modernizing other civilizational spaces, immersing itself instead in the task of understanding new challenges.

The West welcomed the abrupt weakening of Russia but did not believe in the sincerity and fundamental nature of its new Western course, viewing this with indifference.

For this reason, relations between Russia and the West in the 1990s were a complete failure. Under the rule of the reformers-Westernizers, Russia diluted its identity, lost its position in the world, lost its friends, and sacrificed its interests, blindly copying the West without any understanding of the real underlying reasons for its system of values and not even suspecting the true character of post-industrial society or the culture of postmodernity.

The West, for its part, did everything possible to weaken Russia even more, not only not delighting in its new course but also criticizing it in every way and ridiculing its grotesque manner and corrupt criminal substrate. Under these circumstances, not only did Russia not embark on a new round of modernization, but, after destroying old institutions and socio-economic instruments, it also simply adopted separate, uncoordinated fragments of postmodernity, transplanted quick and dirty by elites, oligarchs, and certain segments of the youth subculture.

In the middle of the 1990s, with its territorial integrity in jeopardy (Chechnya), the impression was growing that Russia was entering on a new round of disintegration. The washing away of identity, the absence of a national idea, and the failures of modernization put Russia on the brink of catastrophe. In this situation, the West not only did not help, but also actively furthered the development of destructive tendencies and scenarios.

NATO moved systematically to the East, filling the void that had opened. Networks of agents of influence in Russia continued to indoctrinate the population in the spirit of liberalism and "universal" (read: Western) values. All those who tried to raise the question of the presence of Russia's own national interests were branded "nationalists" or "red-browns."

Today one can say with certainty that relations between Russia and the West in the 1990s were catastrophic for Russia, as they were based on the crudest delusions, categorically incorrect calculations, a complete incomprehension of the real state of affairs, and, in the last analysis, a direct betrayal of national interests.

Before one's eyes, Russia was becoming a colony, with the exogenous, fragmentary intrusion of postmodernity and the gradual loss of sovereignty. The Vice-Speaker of the Duma from "the Union of Right Forces," Irena Khakamada, seriously offered to agree to the international division of labor in a "world government," subject to the conditions of "the transformation of Russia into a nuclear waste depository for more developed countries."

The Strategy of "World Government" in Relation to the USSR and Russia

It is telling that, since the 1980s, the intellectual headquarters of the West, the American "Council on Foreign Relations" (CFR) and its broadened version, "the Trilateral Commission," were striving to draw the Soviet leadership into dialogue, in order to soften the civilizational opposition between "the East" and "the West" with promises of "modernization" and "convergence" and to include part of the post-Soviet elite in their own conceptual pole, on the basis of the specific moral closeness of the Soviet and Capitalist ideologies, emerging from the Enlightenment. These organizations fulfill the function of a laboratory sketch of "world government," which they plan to establish when the West becomes global and "the end of history" arrives. It is important that the basic conceptual game of the CFR with the political leadership of the USSR operated around exactly the complex semantic substance of the concepts of "the West" and "modernity" (the Enlightenment).

Part of the Soviet leadership went along with this, and in the USSR, on the basis of the Institute of Systematic Studies (G. Gvishiani) (a branch of the International Institute for Applied Systems Analysis,

Vienna) a special group of scholars was formed, called on to enter into active dialogue with the intellectual centers of the West. Moscow was practically giving consent to the delegation of its representatives — at first in the guise of scholar-analysts and young economists — to "the world government." It is significant that such actions were supervised by the highest officials in the Central Committee of the Communist Party of the Soviet Union: A. Yakovlev, E. Shevardnadze, A. Primakov. An even greater impression is left by the composition of the "young economists": Y. Gaidar, A. Chubais, G. Yavlinsky, P. Aven. At the Institute of Systematic Studies, Berezovsky, too, begins his career. The members of Chubais' Saint Petersburg circle — G. Glazkov, S. Vasilyev, M. Dimitriev, S. Ignatyev, V. Lyvin, A. Illarionov, M. Manevich, A. Miller, D. Vasilyev, A. Koch, I. Yuzanov, A. Kudrin, O. Dmitrieva — and Gaidar's Moscow circle — K. Kagalovsky, A. Ulyukaev, A. Nechaev, V. Mashits — composed the second eschalon. The majority of participants in this CFR-network occupied future leading roles in the Russian government.

The consequences of the actions of the CFR in the USSR are known. Gorbachev gave the green light to orientation toward "convergence" and Perestroika began. In 1989, a commission of high-standing representatives of the CFR was selected in the Kremlin, with Rockefeller, Kissinger and others at the head. The socialist camp was destroyed, and in 1991 the USSR fell too.

The structures of the CFR in Russia were entirely legalized in 1991 in the form of the Council on Foreign and Defense Policy (Karaganov is officially listed in the supervisory board of the CFR and attends Trilateral Commission panels), while the "young economists" formed the backbone of the Yeltsin government and its ideological nucleus.

In the activities of the CFR network and its Russian affiliates it is easy to deduce how conceptual models operating with the categories of "value," "convergence," "the West," and "the Enlightenment," can actively influence fundamental processes in world politics and destroy a civilizational competitor.

Russia and the West in the Putin Era

Putin's coming to power appreciably corrected this course of the 1990s. The firm directive of the new President for the assertion of national interests was most important. Inasmuch as the biggest threat came specifically from the side of the West — in the first place, the USA and the NATO countries — this had an immediate impact on the increase of international tension.

Putin took the course of strengthening sovereignty and dismantling the structures of external influence, which work through liberal politicians, oligarchs, corrupt officials, and the pro-Western metropolitan intelligentsia.

From this moment, the presence in Russia of its own interests became the indisputable truth, as did the incompatibility of those interests with American or European interests. But Putin, meanwhile, especially in his first Presidential term, repeatedly stated that he "considers Russia a European country," "shares Western values," and is "always inclined to cooperation with the West," especially when "our interests overlap." In other words, he exchanged the Yeltsin model of Russia-West relations ninety degrees. The affirmation of Russia's own interests differed dramatically from the complete submissiveness of the liberal-reformers to the will of the USA, but the idea of integrating Russian into the West, modernizing it along the Western scenario, remained the same.

At the same time, Putin began to pay more and more attention to geopolitics. He clearly distinguished two poles in the structure of the West: the USA and continental Europe. He strove to become closer to Europe to the detriment of the USA. Simultaneously, the United States strengthened the anti-Russian mood in the European Union through Euro-Atlanticism and actively used the countries of New Europe for the establishment of a "sanitary cordon" separating Russian from the European continent. Later, the USA shifted to the tactic of encircling Russia in post-Soviet territory through the organization of "color revolutions" (Georgia, Ukraine, and so on). The geopolitical model of Putin's foreign policy is adequate for international realities: it differentiates policies into European and American orientations.

All of this operates on the level of interests, which is most evidently exhibited in the Russian-European energy partnership: Old Europe is vitally interested in Russian gas and oil and strives towards pragmatic partnership with us; the USA tries to prevent this in all kinds of ways. But on the whole, the historical recognition of Russian interests among the political leadership comes into focus for the first time after the difficult period of the late-Soviet or liberal-reformer delirium and candid betrayal.

Challenge to the West

In his second Presidential term, Putin came to a reassessment and different formulation of the relations of Russia and the West, to the question of values. Repeating assurances of "the correctness of Western values," he began referring to differences in the understanding of democracy, to the national particularities of political systems, to Russian traditions. The timid theory of "sovereign democracy" reflects this changed approach.

On the geopolitical level, in his famous Munich speech Putin exposed to sharp criticism the international politics of the USA and the project of establishing a unipolar world. Essentially, he threw down a challenge to the West as it appears in the present. And here we approach the limit of possible interpretations of the Putin position. While gradually eliminating the unreserved Westernism of the Yeltsin era, Putin remained until the end in the framework of the model "Russia = European country." In the first stage this meant "Russia = a great and sovereign European country with its own interests." Later the position became even more adamantine: "Russia = a great and sovereign European country with its own interests and specific, peculiar values, firmly opposed to American unipolarity." But here is a conceptual contradiction: if "Russia = a great and sovereign European country with its own interests and specific, peculiar values, firmly opposed to American unipolarity," then it is no longer a European country at all, inasmuch as it calls into doubt the universalism of Western values (putting in a claim for their self-sufficient national interpretation) and comes out against the civilizational model of a unipolar world with a West-centric architecture. Furthermore, Russia is not only non-European, but also not even a country, because it simply cannot have its own values, while belonging to a common civilization with other countries. In this case we must speak of civilizations.

It is significant that according to surveys by the Russian Public Opinion Research Centre, taken regularly, 71-73% of Russians in the last ten years persistently answer "Russia is a civilization" to the question "Is Russia, in your opinion, part of Europe or an independent — Orthodox or Eurasian — civilization?" A certain consensus mass (of the nation) is reached in this question. But in the political and higher economic elite, the proportions are clearly different.

The position of Putin in relation to the West — as in a series of other very important political questions — is an attempt to reconcile the elites and the masses. To the masses, he transmits the reference about the independence of Russia; to the elites, he gives assurances of the correctness of the West's course and modernization. We cannot say unambiguously what this is: a conscious tactic to cover up his real position or a fluctuation between these two identities, "Russia as a country" and "Russia as a civilization." If we observe from what and to what Putin moves in his appraisals of the West, then we can suppose that he is either gradually displaying his hitherto veiled Russian civilizational patriotism or actually evolving in this direction under the influence of circumstances and observations concerning the unfolding of events in the international sphere.

The path of newly selected President Medvedev on the whole repeats Putin's basic positions and statements. Medvedev's attitudes toward the West are very similar to Putin's. Medvedev also states that "Russian is a European country," but at the same time, as his predecessor, he insists on national interests (and in part on values) and sharply criticizes the USA and the unipolar world.

CFR Networks in the Putin Period

Despite the considerable correction of the relation to the West in the Putin era, it is rather telling that the basic networks of influence, established back in the 1980s by the West, remain untouched in Russia even in this period. Karaganov and other agents of SWAP continue to be influential figures. Under the aegis of Karaganov, the journal *Russia in Global Affairs*, an affiliate of the American *Foreign Affairs* (the official organ of the CFR), started to be published in 2003 (the main editor: F. Lukyanov). Many on the editorial board of the journal occupy high positions in government, business, political parties and so on. The oligarch Potanin heads the Board of Trustees.

Officially, the "Alpha-Group" — P. Aven and M. Friedman — represents the interests of the CFR in Russia. In its time, by the efforts of this group, the Minister of Defence of the Russian Federation, S. V. Ivanov, and in the Spring of 2008, the Minister of Foreign Affairs of the Russian Federation, S. Lavrov, and even the President of the Russian Federation, D. Medvedev (at the time of the meeting of "the Twenty") visited the headquarters of the CFR in New York. The economic structures of Aven-Friedman (in particular, TNK-VR) are deeply integrated in the American economy, in that segment controlled by the Rockefellers and Morgans, while D. Rockefeller remained for many decades the most important ideologue and sponsor of the CFR (the CFR itself was established by his ancestors, bankers, immediately after the end of the First World War and candidly put as its goal the establishment of a "world government").

These examples show that the evolution of Putin and Medvedev's views concerning relations between Russia and the West do not cross a certain critical line, behind which the presence of networks of influence of "the West" in Russia, in the first place in its highest levels of government, would become intolerable nonsense. This is directly connected to the fluctuation in position of the highest political leadership concerning recognition of Russia as an independent civilization and the acceptance once and for all of the sober and critical view of the West. So long as the President and Premier of Russia continue to assert that Russia is "a European country" (however they might interpret those words), Western structures of influence will exert on the external and internal policies of Russia a great influence, if not an overwhelming one.

Other than the organization of the CFR itself, other organs institutionalizing a similar influence are such platforms as I. Yurgens's Institute for Development (RSPP), the Forum for Strategy-2020, the Higher School of Economics, groups of liberals in the Administration of the President, and so on.

Relations of Russia and the West in the Future

At last, we have come to the final part: to the forecast, wishes, and recommendations concerning the development of future Russia-West relations. The foregoing analysis sought to demonstrate how complex this problem is, how many semantic shifts, nuances, impositions of different values, and geopolitical schemas there are here. The concept and configuration of "the West" are changing. There is no clarity in the definition of Russian identity, and therefore even nuances of definitions and additions to the basic formula can prove to be decisive and to change a plus to a minus, victory to defeat, or vice versa.

Russia stands before a historical dilemma. It needs to work out its relation to the West in a new phase and under new conditions. The situation is aggravated by the deepest economic and, apparently, ideological crisis, which not only the USA but the whole world is going through today, a world so global that a failure of the nuclear West's functioning almost brought down the economy of all other countries, or at least caused them gigantic and irreversible damage. The West became so global that confusions in its center instantly affected the whole periphery.

In order to develop forecasts and strategies for the future development of relations between Russia and the West, it is necessary in the first place to define our concepts.

Perestroika 2: Russia Integrates into the Global "West"

The most theoretically consistent position in this situation would be that of the more radical Westernizers: the West became global, and Russia must accept this while integrating with its structures on any conditions — the earlier, the better. If it is necessary to repudiate sovereignty for such a step, it is worth doing even that, inasmuch as sooner or later globalization will turn authority over to the hands of a supra-national "world government," and one should strive to procure some portfolios in it, instead of becoming involved in a doomed conflict. And if right now the liberal economy is experiencing a crisis, then these problems are only "technical details of the self-regulation of markets"; the market will find a way to get out of the crisis. And insofar as nobody today is offering a distinct alternative to Western liberalism (all the old conflicting variants suffered a bankruptcy), Russia is simply left with no other option but to share the West's hardships.

M. Khodorkovsky reasoned like that, and the members of the opposition party "Other Russia" stand on similar grounds. Most importantly, even more moderate Westernizers, belonging to the network of the CFR and occupying key posts in the Russian economy and partly in the political sphere, hold this point of view in a softened form. Although few people today openly express similar ideas, it is precisely this strategic line that is peculiar to the government's economic block (A. Kudrin, E. Nabiullina, A. Dvorkovich, I. Shuvalov) and to the architects of Russia's international policy, from the Ministry of Foreign Affairs, the Moscow State Institute of International Relations, the President's Administration, Russian oligarchs (in the Russian Union of Industrialists and Entrepreneurs or Jurgens's Institute of Development) and other influential segments of the Russian elite. On the whole, the elite remains faithful to the West, absorbs its values, stores its capital there and settles its families there, spends its free time there and trains its children there. Attitudes toward Putin and Medvedev sharply divide Russian Westernizers in two parts (one for, the other categorically against), but both stem from the principle of the inevitability of globalization and the establishment of a "world government."[8]

One must say that such a position has one important "merit": it allows one to work and live by inertia, without big efforts and labors. The tendencies of globalization and the construction of a unipolar world are developed by the nuclear West both with the help of the inertial untwisting of the flywheel of world history and the intensive work of asserting its interests. The values and interests of the West coincide in their basic character. The movement toward "the end of history" is irreversible; arguments are held only about its speed, phases, and details. However much postmodernism frightened even its adepts, it is written into the logic of social, cultural, technological, and geo-

---

8   This similarity of the positions of the Westernizers for Putin and those against Putin is easy to discover through such examples as the evolution of the opinions of former Prime Minister Kasyanov or Presidential adviser Illarionov, who easily went over to the most radical opposition, but also by attentively learning the list of the editorial council of the pro-American publication, *Russia in Global Politics*, where the radical opposition (Ryzhkov, Khakamada) peacefully live alongside of ministers and high-ranking officials of the President's administration.

political processes; nobody will be able to defer or abolish them by his volitional decree. Thus, Russian Westernizers propose, "to relax and enjoy," even if what is at stake is something unpleasant, or even deadly for the country, for the ambitions of the people, and for Russia's historical mission.

They dispute and ridicule the very presence of this mission, advise the curtailing of ambition, and affirm that unpleasantries can be ironed out constantly by the growing industry of amusement, by the "totalitarian" propaganda of glamour and show business. If Russia dies away as a result of globalization, then, say liberals to comfort us, "there is her hearse"; what is important is only to make this death as unnoticeable and "comfortable" as possible. Russia is dying, but people — if they can, of course — will get the chance to fall in with the global West; they will remain and will probably even be able to make use of newly opened opportunities: freedom of migration, communication, access to knowledge, job search, and an equality of starting conditions.

One must admit that if we think of Russia as a European country, the liberals are right. After all, other European countries gradually repudiate their sovereignty, transfer power — let it be with a whimper — to supra-national agencies (the Brussels bureaucracy), give equal rights to the native population and immigrants from Africa and Asia, erase borders, adopt the English language, and forget about national, cultural, and religious roots. If "Russia is a European country," then, as with other European countries, it needs to prepare to be erased from the face of the Earth, ceding its place to new globalist organizations. For Europe itself, integration is only a temporary stage. If we follow the process of globalization, on its next round the whole world will become a "unified government" (World State), and all peoples and countries will hand power over to the "world leadership" (the embryo of which even now is the CFR or Trilateral Commission).

Such a projected tendency concerning the relations of Russia and the West is not as absurd and marginal as it seems on first glance after that upsurge of patriotic feeling, which grew during the whole of Putin's rule and on the first days of President Medvedev's (especially after August 2008 and the Russia-Georgia conflict). Integration into the global West ("world civilization") is the simplest decision, demanding no effort. The processes of globalization are going by themselves, and even those who do not agree with the values of its ideological content (for instance China and to a lesser degree India), try merely to correct these processes for their own good, to restrict or slow them down somewhat, to give them a definite local color, contesting nuances; but no one — except for radical Islamist circles and the young anarchist movement of the anti-globalists — protests logically and thoroughly against them. From this perspective, to participate in globalization looks not like a volitional choice, but like something self-evident and not demanding a choice, inasmuch as that is made for us by the logic of the history of modernity, the onset of postmodernity, and "the end of history."

Thus, one cannot discard the Westernizer decision offhand. The Soviet regime, more ideologized, radically anti-West, totalitarian, and controlled than the present day regime, collapsed before this inexorable logic of the West and gave up its positions before the convincing arguments of the networks of influence that it itself had established. Wishing to take part in somebody else's modernization at the cost of minimal effort, the USSR paid for its blunder and died. But the shock was quickly forgotten, and before the face of growing problems an analogous approach to things — Perestroika, liberal reforms, closer ties with the USA, entry into NATO, the rejection of gigantic territories and aggravating ethno-sociological regions — could repeat itself entirely, especially in times of increasing trouble. The liberal opposition speaks openly of this. But a significant percentage of the contemporary Russian elite secretly holds the same opinion. For that reason, such a scenario — conditionally speaking, "Perestroika 2" — must not be discounted, even given its low probability due to the contemporary escalation of Russian patriotism.

Russia and the West in Eurasian Theory

By a directly contrary premise, on which one can base a forecast of the development of Russia's relations with the West, the thesis is stated that "Russia is an independent civilization," Russia-Eurasia, a "state-world." In this case, the concept of the West (like modernity and modernization in its various shapes), in practically all the senses of this word, from the historical to the moral and ideological, is taken as evil, as a negative concept, as a Hegelian anti-thesis, as that which one should reject, defeat, overcome, outdo, get rid of, cut short; in the long term, destroy. The Russian Tsars of the Muscovite period held such a view (seeing in Europe the "Kingdom of Heretics," "papists and looters") as did Slavophiles (especially the later ones), Russian *narodniki*, Eurasianists and Communists (in line with their special class ideology).

Proceeding from these Slavophile (Eurasianist) perspectives, relations between Russia and the West must be built in an entirely different spirit. This position can be called strictly anti-Western. Russian (Orthodox-Slavic, Eurasian) civilization must land a last and decisive blow.

This arrangement leads to a complete denial of the path of development of the West and those who found themselves in its zone of influence, willingly or by force (through colonization).

Consequently, the first (and most important) point of strategy becomes a denial of the universality of the historical experience of European civilization, leveling it to a particular case, with a refutation of all its pretensions to being the main path of human development. This implies neither more nor less than a challenge to the whole structure of the epoch of modernity, a repudiation of the Enlightenment, reducing the spirit of modernity to a geographically and historically local phenomenon. If Russia is an independent civilization, then its logic, phases, dynamics, aims, values, and orientation can be utterly different than the path of development and establishment of the West. By whatever paths and whatever logic the West were to go to the end of history, to postmodernity and the post-industrial society, Russia-Eurasia is quite able to say to all of this a decisive "no!" and to refuse it on the basis of its own values, priorities, reference points, choices, and, ultimately, interests.

This position demands a metaphysical reconsideration of Russian identity, the elaboration of the Russian national idea on a new round of its development, in order to bring about under a complete rejection of the West a secure philosophical, paradigmatic foundation. Having stepped onto this path, and not waiting until the huge task of the spirit will be carried out, it is quite possible to sketch out the foundational principles, based on which Russia-Eurasia (as a civilization) will build its relations with the West.

The first and most important point in these relations will be a repudiation of the tendency of the "global West." The West is a local and regional phenomenon, and all its attempts to present itself as a universal standard of development are nothing other than a colonial, racist pretension to absolute power over humanity. A war is declared on the universalism of the West.

Another important conclusion follows from this: modernization, which the West carried out and which it carries to everyone else, is not fate, but a possibility selected voluntarily, which others can either adopt or reject. In this case, modernization transforms into not so much an object of desire as a doubtful adventure, in which society sacrifices religion, ethics, and traditional foundations, but gains technological comfort, raised to the highest value and made the most important criterion. Modernity, with its materialism, atheism and utilitarianism, shows itself as a temptation — attractive, but fatal to the spirit and independence of cultures and peoples. Thus, modernity is deprived of its historical value, while traditional society, including religion, worship, rites, customs and so on, is understood not as something outliving itself, not as inertia and superstition, but as the free choice of a free society.

The West tied its fate to modernity and modernization. If Russia is an independent civilization, different from the West, it may well (and must) act differently, making a choice in favor of traditional society. From this there follows a very important conclusion: Modernity and modernization do not present by themselves absolute values and the unconditional imperative of development. Russia can develop and live in conformity with its internal logic, dictating its own religion, historical mission, and original and distinctive culture.

Russia, understood as a civilization, not only can but must have its own values, differing from other civilizations. Thus, it has a full right to establish its own peculiar political, social, legal, economic, cultural and technological models, ignoring the reaction of the West (and, by the way, of the East).

In concrete policies, these principles turn into the model of the multi-polar world. Moreover, its poles become not segments of the Global West, which only take a pause in order to more effectively built up their societies under a universal standard, but separate civilizations, laying claim to their own understanding of history, their own specific historical time (cyclical or linear), their own ontology, anthropology, sociology, political science, their own world, which others might dislike in vain.

Thus is born the fundamental philosophy of multi-polarity, denying the pretensions of the West to the universality of its way and inviting the peoples of the world themselves to seek not only the means of development, but also to define the goals and direction. If Russia will set out on this path and recognize itself as a civilization (as the overwhelming majority of the population recognize it), this will signify a crusade against the West, denying its universal mission, i.e. casting off modernity and postmodernity as its last expression. This position is not so improbable, though today only Iran, Venezuela, Syria, Bolivia, Nicaragua, North Korea, Belarus, and in a careful manner China take it.

If we allow that the Russian political leadership will take the expected step and proclaim Russia a civilization, a logical chain of practical actions will at once line up:

- Russia will strengthen its relations with those countries that have radically thrown down a challenge to the West, globalization, modernity and postmodernity;
- Russia will begin to split up the West, strengthening its ties with Continental Europe and striving to lead it out from under the control of the USA;
- Russia will establish a filter in relation to the processes of globalization, in the sphere of culture, technology, and values, accepting only that which will promote the strengthening of its strategic power and mercilessly casting aside and outlawing all that weakens, eats away at, and relativizes its civilizational identity;

This kind of turn around will lead to an escalation of tensions with the USA and all the apologists of the "Global West," but will meanwhile attract billions of allies for Russia in those countries that will want to preserve loyalty to their values and traditions, rather than dissolve in a "world government."

Nobody knows the ultimate result of this confrontation, inasmuch as the historical stakes are too great. A genuine battle will break out for the significance of "the end of history" or, according to another outcome, for the continuance of history. If a multi-polar world will be built, history will continue. If not, then postmodernity will ascend to the throne irreversibly, and it will finish, ceding its place to "post-history" (this time, without any gap).

Russia and the West From the Perspective of the Contemporary Russian Government

In order not to give oneself up to empty illusions and not to try to pass the desirable off as the real, it must be stated that today, the Russian government is not at all ready to make a choice either in one or the other direction. Neither Putin nor Medvedev are planning either to dissolve into the West, or to admit that Russia is an independent civilization and to give the West a final fight. Neither the government nor the society is ready for such an abrupt step.

Taking into view the logic of the entire post-Soviet period, it is easy to notice that from unrestrained Westernism the pendulum of Russian politics steadily shifts to the opposite side. The whole history of Putin's presidency, his gigantic rating and the support of his policies among the people are evidence that the self-consciousness of Russians is strongly drawn to the recognition of Russia as a civilization and to the rejection of Westernism. And any suggestion by the government of acting accordingly is immediately taken up with enthusiasm by the broad masses. But, in spite of this, there is an invisible barrier, which holds its evolution in this direction in check. It may be that we are dealing here with the effectiveness of the actions of the agents and networks of influence (in the first place, the CFR). It is possible that there is not yet enough accumulated energy in society to enter into a new round of civilizational struggle, which, in one form or another, Russians waged throughout their entire history.

Whatever the case might be, the position of the current Russian authorities in relation to the West (in its actual embodiment) remains indefinite. The authorities rejected direct Westernism, but also did not take up an alternative (Slavophile, Eurasianist) position. They "stalled," as a computer stalls now and then. They are neither here nor there.

We outlined the general scenarios of the development of relations with the West if the leadership takes one of two fundamental positions:

integration with the Global West, or the assertion of the values and interests of Russia as a civilization in a multi-polar world.

Today, the choice is not made. It is in every way possible put off and set aside. The impression is created that the Russian leaders (Medvedev and Putin) are suffering from the very necessity of this choice, that they would do everything possible for such a strict alternative not to exist, to avoid it by some middle, compromising variant: both West and non-West.

Russia must integrate and modernize, but at the same time preserve sovereignty and independence. Various conceptions like "sovereign democracy" are a desperate effort to reconcile the irreconcilable.

Such indefiniteness and ambiguity are comfortable for a tactical broadening of the field of possibilities. But this is not a resolution of the problem. It is its postponement. This can give (and does give) a positive effect for the reconciliation of Western elites and the Eurasian (nationalist) masses. But sooner or later a choice will have to be made. The Russian authorities are convinced: later is better.

Probably, there are definite grounds for such a position. However, "later" does not mean "never." The moment will come when one will have to give an unambiguous and distinct answer to this dilemma: and so, is Russia a European country or an independent civilization?

When Medvedev speaks of multi-polarity and criticizes the USA, one gets the impression that he has made a choice in favor of civilization. But the next moment, he appears in public in the company of CFR agents of influence and oligarchs and speaks of "democracy and modernization," underscoring the determination of Russia to become a part of the Global West. Putin acted in exactly the same way: he constantly disavowed his own ideological instincts, mixing into one and the same speech the incompatible and mutually exclusive.

This observation shows that the relations of Russia and the West under the current administration will run in an intermediate space between two specific and distinct positions. Rather than the unambiguous "either-or," which would predetermine the long-term logic of Russia-West relations, we are for some time fated to reservation, oscillation, apophasis. The Russian authorities did not ripen for the answer to this fundamental problem. Probably, society itself is not completely ripe for it.

While this compromise exists, we will not await a real and full-fledged decision. But this means that relations between Russia and the West will develop contradictorily and ambiguously: both yes and no. However, the global economic crisis and the logic of globalization, from which the West is not planning to step back, will objectively accelerate (for us) the process of making a decision. It will not work "to stretch the rubber band" past a certain critical point. The authorities will have to make a decision, which will predetermine the logic of the long-term development of relations with the West. It is difficult to anticipate what kind of decision this will be and when it will prevail. But we have tried to describe with the greatest precision among what options a decision will be made.

The Subjective Position of the Author

In this section, my task was to describe as correctly and logically as I could the models of Russia's relations with the West. For that reason, I tried to refrain from journalistic appraisals and the display of personal preferences. Nevertheless, in conclusion I cannot but note that in my opinion:

- Russia is an independent civilization;
- The West and the logic of its becoming is a road to the abyss;
- The claim to the universality of such phenomena as technological progress, democracy, individualism and liberalism conceals racism, cultural superiority and colonial aspirations;

- "Tolerance," propagandized by the West, is a form of the aggressive imposition of its values on all other cultures and civilizations;
- Russia's fate consists in the assertion of its independence, following its own way, the defense of its original values (Orthodoxy, morality, justice, *sobornost'*, holism, and so on), and opposition to the West in all its forms.

CHAPTER 4

Carl Schmitt's Principle of "Empire" and the Fourth Political Theory

The Order of "Large Spaces"

In his 1939 work *The Grossraum* ["large space"] *Order of International Law with a Ban on Intervention for Spatially Foreign Powers: A Contribution to the Concept of Reich in International Law*[9] Carl Schmitt sets forth the basic concept that lies at the foundation of the neo-Eurasianist project in Russia at the start of the 21st century. Although Schmitt wrote his text with regard to Germany at the end of the 1930s, which is reflected in what he discusses there, its significance by far surpasses its historical, political, and geographic context, laying the foundations of a special political-juridical model of thinking, which, most likely, is destined to become a reality only in the 21st century and which has crucial significance for contemporary Russia.

---

9 *The Grossraum Order of International Law with a Ban on Intervention for Spatially Foreign Powers: A Contribution to the Concept of Reich in International Law* (1941), in C. Schmitt, *Writings on War*, trans. by T. Nunan (Cambridge: Polity Press, 2011) pp. 75–124.

The Monroe Doctrine

It is significant that Schmitt himself begins his account of the theory of the "large space" with the "Monroe Doctrine," which was formulated in 1823 by US President James Monroe and became the basis of American foreign policy for two centuries. The sense of the "Monroe Doctrine" boils down to the assertion that the policy of the American continent must by formed by the interests of American states themselves. At the beginning of the 19th century this had a rather concrete sense, since America was then in a semi-colonial situation and European states constantly interfered in its political processes. As the strongest American power, the US took on the responsibility for supporting the independence of the entire American continent from European interference. This is where Carl Schmitt sees the origins of the political theory of the "large space."

"The large space" proceeds from an anti-colonial strategy and proposes (purely theoretically) a voluntary alliance of all countries of the continent, collectively striving to defend their independence. The initiative in the defense of this independence is to be proportionally placed on the stronger powers, from which follows the natural lead of the US. The lead position in securing the independence of the entire American "large space" also signifies recognition of the US's leadership by other countries and the assignment to them of the fundamental burden in the goal of maintaining the freedom of the whole "large space." This in no way suggests that American countries become "provinces" of the US or that they will lose their sovereignty even a little. But inasmuch as they can in practice secure sovereignty on a planetary scale (in the face of colonial European powers) only all together and with the supremacy of the US, the significance of the US grows for all countries, for union with them directly influences the real substance of the sovereignty of each American county.

All of this reflects the realities of the first half of the 19th century, but Schmitt sees in precisely this original form of the "Monroe

Doctrine" something more: the prototype of a balanced and harmonious organization of the whole world in the future; i.e. not a historically conditioned state of affairs, but the optimal project for the future reorganization of the planetary space.

The meaning of the "Monroe Doctrine" consists in the following: the necessity of ensuring the security and independence of one state (the US), conditional upon the strategic status of the adjoining or closely placed powers of the continent. In contrast to Europe, where great states placed close to one another competed among themselves (England, France, Germany, Austria, Italy, Spain, Portugal, Holland, and so on), the US was the sole leader on the American continent and only external, European powers posed a threat. The other American countries were theoretically interested in the same things as the US (in independence from European colonialism), but were not real competitors for it; the extent of their sovereignty was much weaker.

In Europe, the idea that the security of France depends on the political condition of England or Germany would be absurd, since both England and Germany possessed power comparable to France's. European states were compelled to negotiate among themselves for the creation of a general system of security, for instance in the "Concert of Europe," but there were no external threats for all of Europe. When the shadow of such a threat emerged (from Russia or Turkey), temporary alliances among European states sufficed to repulse it.

The US found itself in a principally different situation, and its own safety depended directly on the political situation of other American countries, which, taken by themselves, could not defend their sovereignty and did not represent a real competitor for the US. All this is reflected in the "Monroe Doctrine."

The Juridical Status of the Monroe Doctrine: Politics and the Law, Legality and Legitimacy

Carl Schmitt was a jurist and paid special attention to the legal component of international politics, so he raised the question concerning the legal status of the "Monroe Doctrine." In order to understand Schmitt's assessment, we must recall the fundamental forms of Schmittean analysis.

Schmitt divides the region of law from the region of The Political. He is convinced that law is subordinated to The Political, inasmuch as the initial decision about the formulation, adoption or replacement of a law is always made on the basis of will, going beyond purely legal limits. Schmitt calls this sphere of decision making beyond the domain of the law "The Political." If the law operates with the concept pair "permitted-forbidden," The Political operates with the concept pair "friend-enemy." In contrast to morality, in The Political the determinations "friend-enemy" say nothing about whether we are dealing with "good" or "bad." These concepts have no legal status. An enemy can be noble, just and honorable, but he must be defeated, crushed and destroyed, as he is an enemy.

Following Max Weber, Schmitt also distinguishes "legality" and "legitimacy." Legality is correspondence to a strictly determinate and fixed legal code. Legitimacy is the total and general correspondence of one or another political action or decisions to the opinion of the majority, the people, society. Politics and law, legality and legitimacy are closely connected with each other and to differentiate between them in specific instances is difficult. Only in a critical situation ("a state of emergency") does their nature become fully apparent, because The Political comes forward of itself, displaying its essential superiority over the legal. Here, too, the concept of legitimacy becomes apparent and the potential of sovereignty comes into force.

Applying these concepts to the "Monroe Doctrine," one can say that Americans themselves regarded it as entirely legitimate, belonging to the essence of The Political, and emerging from a sovereign decision to secure the sovereignty of the US, and the whole American continent besides, properly.

"The Monroe Doctrine" is the quintessence of American foreign policy. It determined who is a friend and who is an enemy. Friends were all the American countries; enemies, the great European states with their colonial encroachments upon the New World. In order to defend its sovereignty against "the enemy," a decision was made to consider the entire territory of America a single strategic space. The Americans (at least the American political class) perceived this as an entirely legitimate phenomenon. "The Monroe Doctrine" did not acquire legal-juridical status, but this only added flexibility, inasmuch as it allowed its goals to be more successfully realized in practice.

The essence of The Political was exhibited in full measure in the "Monroe Doctrine." In that moment the US made a historical decision concerning their world status. The thesis "America for Americans" had in that moment a rather concrete meaning: "for Americans, but not for Europeans" ("not for Europeans" as external, controlling powers).

The Evolution of the "Monroe Doctrine"

Schmitt noticed a change in the sense of the "Monroe Doctrine" already in the 19th century, when the US began to use it as a cover for colonial policies inside the continent. True, in comparison with the open colonialism of the European states, the colonialism of the US remained relative; it took place under the guise of "the spread of democratic values"; i.e. in the eyes of the citizens of the US themselves it was a civilizing and liberating activity. Schmitt himself figured that if there was a departure from the original content, it was for the time being insignificant, because the priority of the US in the framework of the "Monroe Doctrine" can theoretically be interpreted rather broadly.

A much more important shift in the doctrine occurred at the start of the 20th century when US Presidents Roosevelt and Wilson especially proposed to interpret it separately from historical and geographical realities and to ground with its help the necessity of the US's participation in world problems for the "strengthening of democracy, rights and freedoms." Here "the Monroe Doctrine" clearly passes beyond American borders and transforms into a universalistic, planetary theory, supporting a new type of colonialism: not European (open, straightforward, and cynical), but American (concealed by the civilizing and ideological function of spreading liberal-democracy). The English, too, tried to apply the "Monroe Doctrine" in this universalistic-hegemonic and ideological form to their global empire, having asserted as an international principle the necessity of English global control over channels, inasmuch as the security (economic, hence also political and military) of England directly depends on it.

From an anti-colonial theory connected with a concrete "large space," in the 20th century the "Monroe Doctrine" started to transform into a universalistic, ideological theory of a new type of planetary colonialism (sea-based, English, and especially American).

For the Americans and English themselves this was also a political decision, a distribution of the functions of friends and enemies, and it was based on internal legitimacy. But for continental European states — Germany, France, Russia — and also for certain awakening governments of Asia (Japan), this promulgation of the "Monroe Doctrine" was categorically unacceptable, hostile and illegitimate.

After the victory over Germany in the First World War and the revolution in Russia, on the grounds of the new interpretation of the "Monroe Doctrine" and under the dictation of England and the US, an attempt was made to build up a system of international law (the League of Nations). This system received the name of Versailles. It is very important to understand how it is connected with the "Monroe Doctrine."

The countries of the Entente act here as subjects of sovereignty (first of all England, France and the US), and the territory controlled by them on both sides of the Atlantic Ocean is taken as the collective center. The rest of the world is regarded as the periphery, from which threats can arise, and consequently, it was not permitted to allow even one of the countries belonging to the periphery to acquire power. Under the aegis of England, France and the US, The League of Nations was called to be for the entire world what the US was for the American mainland: a guarantor of security against enemies. But if in the original version of the "Monroe Doctrine" the European countries were the enemies, henceforth they became pariahs: Weimer Germany, young Soviet Russia, militaristic Japan, and so on. Other countries, unable to defend their sovereignty independently in the face of the likely aggression of "pariahs," were offered to adopt the protectorate of Western states in the framework of the League of Nations.

Thus, the "Monroe Doctrine" tore itself away from a concrete "large space" and became the foundation of a planetary, universalistic model of a world order. Moreover, it lost its defensive function and transformed from an instrument of war with colonialism into colonialism (of a new ideological, liberal-democratic type).

Carl Schmitt shows that the architects of Versailles attempted to impart to the new version of the "Monroe Doctrine" (in Woodrow Wilson's interpretation) a legal-juridical status, but because of regional contradictions, this was not done. Nevertheless, for the Versailles world order and the era of the League of Nations this was the fundamental legitimate model, expressing The Political and determining the structure of sovereignty.

After the Second World War, this same model lay at the foundation of the NATO bloc. Defeated Germany and Japan were included in the "space of the West," while the USSR and the countries of the Soviet bloc became the main enemy.

The Large Space and "*Reich*" in Schmitt's Understanding

Carl Schmitt wrote his work on the eve of the Second World War, and he was interested in trying to understand the picture that he saw. Pragmatically, he substantiated the foreign policy of Nazi Germany. Theoretically, he tried to understand the political picture of foreign policy. Schmitt resolves both of these problems in the text that we are investigating.

Distinguishing in the "Monroe Doctrine" two rather remote senses (the original, connected with a concrete "large space," and the deformed, ideological-imperialistic "Versailles" type), Schmitt contrasts them with one another. Moreover, he applies to the original version of the "Monroe Doctrine" the scientific term "large space" and "the order of large spaces," on the basis of which he proposes to build a system of international law.

He underscores that in the concept "large space" both terms have not a quantitative (natural scientific), but qualitative, historical and, if you wish, sacred content. "Large" refers not only to physical dimension, but also to the level of internal organization, consolidation, mastery, and integration of the expanse into a social-cultural, civilizational, strategic, and political unity. This is the very sense in which we make use of the concept "great." "Space" [*Raum, prostranstvo.* Translated elsewhere as "territorial space"] is also thought of not as an abstract category of physics, but as a concrete landscape — woods, fields, mountains, rivers, and knolls, forming the environment of the being of *peoples* and races. In this sense, the concept "large space" directly approaches the concept "Empire" (the German word "*das Reich*" signifies "empire," "kingdom").

Russian Eurasianists employed the expression "state-world" (Savitsky). This formula, "state-world," incidentally, also contains the ambiguity that Schmitt detected in the "Monroe Doctrine." Savitsky understands "state-world," "empire," as a concrete part of the world space, representing a civilizational unity (this is the foundation of Eurasianism). It was so in the original version of the "Monroe Doctrine." But if one steps back from Savitsky's concrete Eurasianist meaning, the same expression can be interpreted as globalism, i.e. the concept of "world state," "world government." This is exactly what happened in the Versailles era and with the creation of The League of Nations and was later reflected in the establishment of NATO, the world order of the "Trilateral Commission," and contemporary American-centric globalism.

Universalism (globalism) operates with a physical picture of the world. The "large space" works with a historical and sacral one. The subject of universalism is the individual (the liberal theory of "human rights"). For the theory of "large space," the subject is the concrete, organic collective that is the *narod* [*Volk*, people. Most often transliterated in the singular as a technical term and translated "peoples" when plural. The adjectival form has been translated "popular" or "ethnosocial" depending on context. Dugin discusses the category of *narod* in detail in his book *Ethnosociology*]. That is why Carl Schmitt connects the concepts "human rights" and "large space." The essence of the two contrasting notions of world order are reflected here: multi-polar and unipolar, concrete-historical and universal, founded on a few "empires" ("Reichs," in Schmitt's term) or representing together one empire (in our case, the American: the role the US played in the framework of the original "Monroe Doctrine" in the 19th century in relation to the American continent and began to play in the 20th century together with the NATO countries in relation to the whole world).

In 1939 Schmitt himself saw the Third Reich precisely as an "Empire," a "large space," a "state-world." And he tried to justify such a role for Germany. The Third *Reich* as a "large space" was for Schmitt not so much a German as a European concept. He saw in it the expression of continental European civilization in its classical (and not Enlightenment) expression (Schmitt was an ardent Catholic and conservative). He understood the National-Socialist government as the core of the peoples of Europe, not as a new colonial power or national government. Hence also his attitude toward "the rights of peoples." Although a supporter of Hitler, Schmitt never agreed in his texts with the racist and narrowly German interpretation of the "*Reich*." By "*Reich*" Schmitt meant the common initiative of all European peoples, and although historically the Western Roman empire was established on the basis of German tribes, for Schmitt all European *ethnoses* participated in a common imperial history and should have identical rights in the future.

Schmitt's National Socialism fundamentally differs from the National Socialism of Hitler or Rosenberg precisely in that Schmitt thinks in the category of peoples, not of one people, the German, or the notorious "Aryan Race," by which ignorant Nazis understood only Germans themselves. He thinks in the categories of the "large space," in the categories of a harmonious co-existence of different empires (including the "Russian-Soviet," "Eurasian"), and not of German colonization. Precisely for that reason in 1936 the journal *Schwarze Korps* published a denunciation of Schmitt, costing him his career. But Schmitt was never an opportunist and continued to develop his ideas even as a "dissident," as did many "conservative revolutionaries" displaced onto the periphery or even subjected to persecution by zealous dilettantes and weak-headed Nazi fanatics.

In the work we are investigating, it is remarkable that Schmitt continues to use the expression "the rights of peoples" at the very peak of Hitler's racist policies, which recognized only Germans as of full value. Schmitt's "Third *Reich*," (exactly like the "Third *Reich*" of the author of this concept, Arthur Moeller Van Den Bruck) is a different "*Reich*" from Hitler's. It is an "empire," a "large space," inhabited by peoples, each of which has equal rights in the creation of The Political and participates in its own fate. And the central authority, the center of the empire, is called on in the first place to secure all peoples from the interference of extra-spatial powers (this is spoken of in the very title of the examined text). In his policies, Hitler committed the same mistake as both the US and the English Imperialists, who moved from a concrete "large space" to universalism and globalism, except that the latter took as a shield the liberal-democratic ideology, while Hitler took as a shield racist doctrines and the idea of a "global Aryan government," no less absurd and deleterious than the ideology of human rights.

If we attend more carefully to Schmitt's ideas (more broadly, to the ideas of conservative revolutionaries, including Oswald Spengler, Ernst Von Salomon, Otto Petel, Arthur Moeller Van Den Bruck, Franz Shauwecker, Ernst and Friedrich Jünger, Herman Wirth, Friedrich Hielscher, and Martin Heidegger), we will easily discover that we are dealing with the Fourth Political Theory (alongside liberalism, communism and fascism), which was concealed by the Third (the Nazi and Fascist variants). The tragedy of the idea is that this Fourth Political Theory, historically overshadowed by the Third, at some point entered into solidarity with it, not having survived an ideological war on three fronts (together with polemics against liberals and communists, conservative revolutionaries had to deal with misrepresentations of their own ideas in vulgar Nazism).

Much can be written about the natural feeling of German patriotism and the fact that Germany was compelled to oppose not only their main and legitimate enemies, the liberal-democratic English but also Soviet expansion from the East. Some (including Schmitt himself) tried to act from within the regime, in order to reinterpret Hitler's suicidal course in the spirit of the "rights of peoples" and the "large space." But as a result the Fourth Theory turned out to be buried under the ruins of the Third *Reich*, which historically remained the *Reich* of Adolf Hitler, and not the "*Reich*" of Carl Schmitt.

The Soviet "Large Space" or Russian *Reich*

The model of the "large space" is ideally suited for an analysis of Russia's Soviet period. The Russian Eurasianists developed this theme completely independently. They also operated with the central category of the "large space." Savitsky introduced the term "place-development" for this analysis. As also for Schmitt, for the Russian Eurasianists the fundamental enemies were the liberal countries of the West, although the Eurasianists themselves included Germany in the composition of the West at the same time as Schmitt supposed it to be the center of the European continent, while "the West starts beyond the Rhine."

Those same Eurasianists foretold with absolutely perfect precision the evolution of Soviet foreign policy from the internationalism of the first years to the full-fledged imperial policies of the late 1920s. The USSR was a classical example of the large space, which, in Schmitt's terminology, could well be called the "Soviet *Reich*." The proper term is "Eurasia," introduced by the Eurasianists and called upon to underscore the organic unity of the "large space" of the Eurasian mainland, corresponding to Russia's borders, from ancient Russ to the USSR. Moreover, in contrast to the ideological manner of thinking of the Bolsheviks and leaders of the USSR, who based their theories on Marxism, where nothing is said either of territorial space, tradition, or civilizations, the Eurasianists interpreted the USSR as a historical-spatial, civilizational, and geopolitical organism, and not only as an ideological construction. Precisely their analysis of Soviet history, especially applicable to the Stalinist period, proved most correct and accurate among all other émigrés. Eurasianists evaluated the USSR almost as Schmitt evaluated Hitler's Third *Reich*. They saw through the Soviet façade the deep logic of the "large space," the legitimacy of an eternal "empire," the dialectic of the Third Rome, and the historical sovereignty of the Russian *narod*, delivered to the political elite (in this instance to the Bolsheviks) with one order: to safeguard the country and peoples from the interference of external-spatial powers. And the Bolsheviks carried out this task over the course of seventy years.

Essentially, Eurasianists were the representatives of the Fourth Political Theory, as were the German conservative revolutionaries. But they discerned its elements not behind Fascism (The Third Political Theory), but behind the Second Political Theory. Ustryalov analyzes this in a particularly detailed manner.

The idea of building socialism in one country with regard to Russia was already a turn to the "large space" and the legitimacy of the *"Reich."* If the power of the Fourth Political Theory in Nazi Germany and the USSR would have proven decisive, while superficial ideological arguments would have retreated to a place of secondary importance, we would have had a completely different world: ideal (within the framework of the possible), multi-polar, and balanced. We see an unrealized (aborted) sketch of the purely theoretical victory of the Fourth Political Theory in the Ribbentrop-Molotov Pact and in the conception of a different conservative revolutionary Karl Haushofer, "the Berlin-Moscow-Tokyo axis."

The New Relevance of the Fourth Political Theory

Now we will move on to the present. The legacy of Carl Schmitt has become today an inalienable component of the political and juridical culture of the Western elite. As was made clear, it surpassed by far its concrete historical situation and penetrated into fundamental problems that have not at all lost their relevance even today but have, on the contrary, only gained relevance. But if we look a little more broadly, it becomes understandable that we are dealing not only with Schmitt himself and his personal legacy. In fact, the significance of the Fourth Political Theory, of which Carl Schmitt was an impressive representative but far from the only one, is growing dramatically.

In our time, only liberalism survived out of the three fundamental political theories of the 20th century. Fascism disappeared; communism has almost disappeared. In any case, it is not possible to relate to either one or the other seriously. Not only because they lost historically — that is only half the matter — but also because they became ideologically bankrupt. Those who believed in them were not only crushed; they were humbled and disgraced on a theoretical level. Today, neither fascists nor communists can distinctly explain the reasons for their fall, and precisely for that reason there are none of them not only in the present but also in the future. Fascist thought came to nothing; Marxist thought in its pure state is vanishing. Where it exists at all, it joined without fail with other foreign ideological tendencies (national tendencies in Asia and the Third World and liberal tendencies in European social-democracies). The Fourth Political Theory, to which the ideas of the "large space," "empire," "the rights of nations," "organic democracy," "multi-polarity," "place-development," "geopolitical sovereignty," and "geopolitics," relate, on the other hand, continues to prove its strength. Before our eyes, precisely it is becoming the sole reasonable and well-founded alternative to globalism, "human rights," unipolarity, liberal-democratic universalism, individualism, and the totalitarianism of the market and market values.

Schmitt foresaw a world consisting of "empires," "large spaces," and "*Reichs.*" Applying his views to actuality, we can well distinguish in the future an Atlantic "Empire" (with its center in the US), an Asian "Empire" (China and Japan), a European "Empire" (corresponding to Schmitt's idea), and, finally, a Eurasian "Empire."

Schmitt saw himself as an observer of the European Empire and looked at the world from the perspective of the European *Reich*. Eurasianists elaborated the grounds of an analogous worldview, but they did so while looking at the world from Russia. The Japanese model of the reorganization of the Pacific Ocean into a "large space" was interrupted by defeat in the Second World War, and today China is attempting to play the leading role in this process. Russia just recently lost an enormous segment of its "large space," but it is gradually orienting itself in a Eurasian direction (which suggests a new phase of integrational initiatives).

If three potential "large spaces" (the European, Eurasianist and Asian) are due for an expansion, in order to become "Empires," "*Reichs*," then the Atlantic expanse, which lays claim today to universality and global scope, will have to contract. In order that the US returns anew to the original version of the "Monroe Doctrine," in order that it again becomes a "large space" and an "Empire," its influence must be appreciably curtailed.

Such an analysis shows that Carl Schmitt's theory of "large spaces," as a graphic expression of all the constructions of the Fourth Political Theory, is the most secure platform for a multi-polar world, anti-globalism, anti-Americanism and the national-liberation struggle against American global dominance.

A consideration of Carl Schmitt's text *The Grossraum Order of International Law with a Ban on Intervention for Spatially Foreign Powers: A Contribution to the Concept of Reich in International Law*, freed from historical conditions, together with the other fundamental texts of both Schmitt and other conservative revolutionaries, represents an inalienable part of the legacy of neo-Eurasianist theory and helps one to better understand the meaning of neo-Eurasianism, the contemporary expression of the Fourth Political Theory, reformulated in conditions of the 21st century by Russians, in Russia, in the interests of Russia and for the flourishing of Russia as a world power.

Neo-Eurasianism is the political theory of the construction of Empire, of a "large space," in the present and the future. Either Neo-Eurasianism will become the fundamental paradigm of the Russian elite, or an occupation awaits us. Let us notice that other potential "large spaces" and other peoples are all without exception interested in an Eurasianist renaissance starting in Russia. Everybody wins from this, since Eurasianists speak up strongly not for universalism, but for "large spaces," not for imperialism, but for "empire," not for the "interests of any one people," but for "the rights of peoples."

CHAPTER 5

The Project "Empire"

Empire without an Emperor

There exists the opinion that the concept of Empire necessarily presupposes the presence of an emperor. However, an unprejudiced analysis of this phenomenon shows that history knows a multitude of empires without emperors. Some of them were directed by a limited circle of elected aristocrats; others, by a parliament or senate. Consequently, the presence of a sole monarchical power, an emperor, is not a necessary condition for the existence of an empire. Moreover, there were many monarchical, despotic, tyrannical, or dictatorial governments, with the absolute power of the Tsar or authoritarian leader, which were not called empires and had nothing in common with them. Thus, we can well consider the principle of empire in complete independence from the emperor.

Empire as the Optimal Instrument for the Making of Civil Society

Another popular confusion is that empire is an extremely archaic phenomenon, which was already overcome by contemporary civilization on the threshold of modernity. This, too, is far from true. On the contrary, both ancient and modern empires were a form of political organization that by technological, ideological, social, administrative and economic parameters by far excelled the societies that had preceded the rise of these empires.

Empires practically always signified the modernization of the peoples, societies, and governments that fell within their borders. They established on enormous expanses a general social and legal way of life, unified and opened particular ethnic communities for an intensive dialogue with all others, promoted technological development, facilitated trade and other forms of cultural exchange, and created the preconditions for the development of civil society.

In particular, the Roman Empire after the edict of the Emperor Caracalla recognized a right to Roman citizenship for all free people who found themselves at that time under Roman rule, although earlier the right of citizenship was available only to certain distinguished men of the local elite. For instance, the apostle Paul, Saul in his days as a noble Jew, had Roman citizenship long before the edict of Caracalla.

Although they were established on the rejection of empire, contemporary European nation-states copied entirely the system of citizenship from precisely the imperial model. And it is not surprising that precisely Roman law, reflecting the legal logic of the establishment of empire, lies at their foundation in the present.

The Definition of Empire

If empire is defined neither by the presence of an emperor, nor by its belonging to an archaic political system, then what marks are objectively inherent to it? How are we to define empire?

Empire is a kind of political-territorial arrangement that combines a strict strategic centralism (a single vertical line of power, a centralized model of administration by armed forces, the presence of a general civil legal code, a single system of tax collection, and unified system of communication, and so on), with the broad autonomy of the regional social-political establishments entering into its composition (the presence of elements of ethnic-confessional rights on a local level, multinational composition, a broadly developed system of local self-government, and the possibility of the co-existence of different local models of power, from tribal democracy to centralized principalities or even kingdoms).

Empire always lays claim to a universal scope, recognizing its political system as the core or synonym of global empire. "All roads lead to Rome." All empires think of themselves as global empires. Empire is endowed with a mission. It is perceived as the political embodiment of the historical fate of humanity. The mission can be realized in religious (Byzantium, Austro-Hungary, the Islamic Caliphate, the Muscovite Tsardom), civic (Ancient Rome, the Empire of Ghengis-Khan), civilizational (the Chinese empire, Iranian Empire) or ideological (the Communist Empire of the USSR, the Liberal Empire of the USA) forms.

In this generalized political and social sense, Empire and its principles acquire a special relevance for our time, too.

The Empire of the Neo-Cons (Benevolent Empire)

The thesis concerning the relevance of the term "Empire" for the comprehension of the realities of today's world confirms the upsurge of interest in this concept in the global political discourse of the 21st century. Starting from 2002, the broad American press started to use this term with regard to the role that the US should play with respect to the rest of the world in the new century (possibly millennium). In American society a fierce argument arose about empire. As is always the case in such arguments, this concept was understood differently in different circles, but the concept itself became central.

To a certain extent, this process was a consequence of the almost undivided influence in American politics of the neoconservatives during the era of the younger Bush. Starting from the Reagan formula of the "USSR as the Empire of Evil," the theoreticians of this school proposed a symmetrical project: the US as the "Empire of Good," the "benevolent empire" (Kagan).

Neo-conservatives thought of the role of the US in the 21st century as the function of a global integrator, as a new (postmodern) Rome. In such a project, all the signs of empire were immediately evident:

- Centralized, strategic management of the world (by the USA and NATO)
- Global ideology (liberal-democracy);
- Uniform model of the economy (the market);
- Determinate autonomy of regional vassals (having some degree of freedom in their domestic policies, but compelled to follow strictly behind American lines in fundamental questions);
- Planetary scope (planetary civil society, globalization, One World);
- Mission of democratization and liberalization of all the countries and nations of the world.

In a burst of enthusiasm at the start of the 1990s, Francis Fukuyama called the establishment of a global American empire "the end of history." A little later he admitted that he had rushed and that a global American empire is still not yet a done deal, but only a project and distant goal, on the path to which serious difficulties, delays and, possibly, tactical retreats can arise.

Samuel Huntington, another American political scientist, summarized the totality of these objections in his no less epochal book, showing that the establishment of a global American "empire of good" will be blocked by "the clash of civilizations." Huntington concluded that the path to the global scope of the USA must be gradual, that in the given moment it is more important to rally the Atlantic core (the USA and the countries of NATO) and, while manipulating civilizational antagonisms, to wait for an advantageous moment in the future. But in any case the thesis that the USA is the empire of the 21st century is generally accepted in American political discourse, however the historical timelines and territorial borders of its establishment are understood.

The American political elite thinks today with the categories of empire. Moreover, they do this independently of whether or not the representatives share the optimistic and aggressive ideas of the neo-conservatives. The harsh critic of the neoconservatives and "democrat" Zbigniew Brzezinksi is a supporter of American empire no less than Dick Cheney, Richard Perle, Paul Wolfowitz, or William Kristol.

Negri and Hardt's Criticism of "Empire"

The term "empire" has become popular today not only in the American establishment. Extreme leftist philosophers and anti-globalists, the ardent opponents of capitalism, liberal-democracy and the US, actively use it and even make it a synonym of their main ideological project. The theoretician of the "Red Brigades" Antonio Negri and the American philosopher and anti-globalist Michael Hardt wrote the work *Empire*, which, in their opinion, must become the analogue of Marx's *Capital* for the global leftist movement of the 21st century. This is a kind of "Bible" of anti-globalism.

Negri and Hardt describe US history as originally combining in itself the principle of network organization with imperial messianism, which in their opinion made precisely the US the world leader, establishing planetary authority in the form of a moral, economic, and socio-political order obligatory for all.

By "empire" Negri and Hardt understand the establishment of a global state, based on capitalist exploitation by "the authorities" of the creative potential of "the masses" under the central role of the USA, which will gradually transform into a world government. For Negri and Hardt, a world empire is the apotheosis of the preceding stages of the development of capitalism and the height of injustice and exploitation. This is the worldwide "society of the spectacle" (Guy Debord). This world empire is regarded as the empire of postmodernity, where power and violence acquire not an open but a veiled, network character.

The authors themselves propose to treat this situation as a historical chance for the "many" to carry out a world revolution. Empire blends classes and peoples, countries and political systems, into a cosmopolitan pot. Only exploiters (the world government, operators of the network empire) and the "many," devoid of any qualities, and consequently being the ideal "proletariat" of the 21st century, remain. According to Negri and Hardt, "the many" must find a way — through narcotics, all kinds of perversions, genetic engineering, cloning and other forms of bio-intellectual mutations — to slip away from the power of empire and to undermine it from within, using for its anarchic-demolishing actions the opportunities that empire itself opens up.

Thus, the category of "empire" becomes the cornerstone of the ideological constructs of the global leftist movement, anti-globalism and alter-globalism. In fact, alter-globalism is the direct consequence of Negri and Hardt's ideas: one must not fight with globalization, but rather use its capitalistic and imperialist forms (existing today) for an anti-capitalistic revolutionary war.

Alternatives to Global Empire: The Extension of the Yalta-Based Status Quo

If we take the project of the global American empire seriously, the question quickly emerges: what can be proposed as an alternative? We've already familiarized ourselves with one alternative, but it is attractive for a limited number of far leftists: Trotskyists, anarchists, postmodernists. Let's look at some other projects.

The simplest answer to the imperial project will be the wish to preserve the status quo. This is the instinctive wish to leave inviolable that international order which was formed in the 20th century, where sovereignty is tied to nation-states and the forum for the decision of controversial international questions is the UN. Such an approach is waning, inasmuch as the world order of the 20th century after 1945 took shape along the outcome of the Second World War and the nominal sovereignty of nation-states was supplied by the parity of the strategic arms of the two superpowers, the US and the USSR. The imperial ambitions of one group (the socialist camp) were equalized by the imperial ambitions of the other (the capitalist camp). The remaining states were invited to fit into this balance with a wide area for maneuvers in the movement of non-aligned countries. The UN only secured this balance in the structure of the Security Council.

After the break-up of the Soviet camp and the fall of the USSR the entire system of the Yalta-based world collapsed, strategic parity was broken and practically all states were compelled to bring their sovereignty into correlation with the disproportionately increased power of the American empire. The UN ceased to have any significance, and the Yalta-based world order became a thing of the past.

Many countries were not completely aware of this global transformation and continue to think by habit in the categories of yesterday's world, when two competing empires (the Soviet and the American) acted as guarantors of sovereignty for all other countries. After Yalta there remained one empire, and not to notice this is merely to postpone the realization, unpleasant for many, of the real state of affairs.

The countries that tried to object to this unipolar picture — Iraq, Yugoslavia, Afghanistan — felt on their hides what the post-Yalta world is and what the price of sovereignty is in it. The problem is that in the conditions of the 21st century no state can defend its sovereignty against a direct, head-on conflict with American empire, especially when the other leading countries of the world stand on the side of the US. The technological complexities that Americans face in the matter of planetary empire-building (and this is globalism on its different levels), should not lead us into confusion: if something is not working out for them, this does not mean that it will not work out.

The project of building a global liberal-democratic empire is the main and sole plan of American foreign policy in the 21st century, and after the break-up of the bipolar world, there is nothing formally with the power to challenge this model. Optimists and pessimists in the US argue over when the empire will be established — tomorrow or the day after — but not whether it is worth establishing it at all. And these are important arguments. The fact that many states do not want to part with their sovereignty represents a purely psychological problem: this is something like phantom limb pain, torturing the owner of the already absent limb.

No state in today's world can principally defend its sovereignty before the face of the global empire in mid-term and long-term perspectives. The most that can realistically be done is to delay it. But delay is not an alternative. States today are sovereign only nominally and are not alternatives to the unipolar world. In this situation, the UN is doomed to atrophy, as Washington constantly reminds us.

The Islamic Empire (The Global Caliphate)

If no single state has enough potential to block the onset of the American (Atlantic) empire in the contemporary world, there remains only one choice: either to surrender to the mercy of the victor and to cling to the jackboots of the new owner of the world (as, by the way, do many countries of Eastern Europe and the CIS) or to give some kind of asymmetrical answer (the anarcho-Trotskyist variant in the spirit of Negro-Hardt we leave for the parlor games of the postmodernists and marginal groups, drug addicts and perverts).

It is exceedingly important not merely to realize on what resources, in the material sense, this alternative can operate, but also what ideology to take as the integrating factor. One such ideological answer is contained in the project of fundamentalist Islam. In its political expression it opposes to the global American empire another empire, the global Islamic Caliphate, and this is entirely logical. The character of the opposition is factored into the Islamic project: to a global challenge a global (albeit asymmetrical) response is given.

In the confrontation between the US and "Al-Qaeda," however strange and disproportionate such a duel of the leading world state with extraterritorial "international terrorism" might seem, we are dealing with a clash of equally great ideological projects. Islamic fundamentalism proposes:

- The establishment of a global Islamic government;
- The wide autonomy of ethnic groups, which will be obliged to undergo Islamization or to pay a tithe (as "people of the book");
- The introduction of the standards of Islamic economics (rejection of interest, the deduction of a tithe for the benefit of the community and the Ummah, with a subsequent distribution among the poor);
- A religious mission (Islam and Islamization);
- A planetary scale (Muslims live in all parts of the world).

As an answer to American globalization, the Islamic project falls under the definition of Empire. Of course, there is a question here concerning the resources of the opposition. But postmodernism with its network society (Castells) comes to the help of the Islamists. The latter use the poverty of Muslims recruited for international terrorist acts, exploit religious potential driven to fanaticism, set religious and ethnic groups in all parts of the world into motion for the founding of their own networks, use the internet and other information technologies to wage an informational war and, finally, resort to terrorist acts, as in the case of September the 11th, 2001, which already brings a quite tangible blow to that empire, against which a war is being fought. The declaration by Islamic radicals that their major adversary is the US is a sufficient proof that we are dealing with a serious and important project: the project of an alternative world empire.

The European Union: A Teetering Empire

The European path — much less determinate and softer — is different. United Europe has two geopolitical identities: on the one hand, it is the outskirt of the American empire, used as a place for the accommodation of American military bases, and on the other hand, it is the germ of an alternative geopolitical formation with its own system of interests and priorities, which can rather differ (sometimes even essentially) from the American ones. Thus, one should speak not of one Europe, but of two, which are superimposed one on the other.

There is an Atlantic Europe and a Continental Europe. Continental Europe, also called "Old Europe," whose core, it will be recalled, is France and Germany (both Italy and Spain are strongly attracted to them), for now represents the unrealized project of independent empire. This European empire, existing as a historical draft, made itself known at the time of the American invasion into Iraq, when there was almost a Paris-Berlin-Moscow axis as the embryo of an independent political formation, called on to restrain the establishment of a unipolar American world.

Very recently, by the endeavors of continental Europe, Ukraine's and Georgia's ascension into NATO was halted. Too dependent on the US in strategic arrangements, and to a large extent sharing values (democracy, liberalism, the market, human rights, technological development) with the Americans, Europe does not bring itself to resolve its imperial projects straightforwardly. We only guess at them. Moreover, the other Europe, the Atlantic one, the pillars of which are pro-American England and the countries of New Europe, lacks a European self-consciousness and is on the whole dependent on the US. It strives to undermine the project of European (mainly, Franco-

German) empire and preserve the EU as a zone of direct American control.

Europe's duality shows in everything. Thus, there is no success in making a choice between two imperial projects, the conformist American one, and the other, alternative (if you like, "revolutionary") European one, the continental one. But meanwhile one should take into account that the majority of Europeans soberly realize that as a minimum they can be competitors (to say nothing of strategic independence) only as the European Union, and by no means as states. In other words, that Europe is compelled to move to imperial forms of political organization is a settled question. Taken separately, even the biggest countries of Old Europe cannot defend their national interests. Whether Europe will ever become an independent empire or whether it will remain the periphery of Atlanticism, it is doomed to integrate.

Russian "Defeatists"

Now we must speak of Russia, too. How should we, Russians, work out the conditions of the 21st century? This problem unfolds into a few components. First, everything must begin with an answer to the challenge of the unipolar world. Simply speaking: how do we relate to the American empire?

If we are aware of what the American empire is, then we must be determined to equalize sovereignty. The very fact of globalization and the American unipolar world signifies a decrease of our sovereignty, up to its final abolishment (with the transfer of fundamental strategic functions to the imperial center). Either Russia's sovereignty or the global American empire: that is the dilemma.

There are two positions here. One consists in admitting the defeat of the USSR as something irreversible, hoisting the white flag (of treason), and attempting to take up a more comfortable role in the new American empire. This is how reformers in the Yeltsin era thought; this is how liberal and "democratic" forces (SPS, Yabloko), the hosts of

"Echo Moscow," many Russian oligarchs (Khodorkovsky proclaimed this more clearly than others), and participants in the radical opposition ("Other Russia," Kasyanov, Kasparov, etc.) continue to think.

One must say that such a position, despite its moral defectiveness (after all, it signifies a direct betrayal of our national interests), works with cold facts. The US has both the ideology of a new empire and significant resources for its realization. The opponents of globalization have emotions, extravagant models of the Negri-Hardt type and the ominous terrorist project of fundamentalist Islam (unattractive, it must be said). Meanwhile, there are almost no convincing resources to disrupt assuredly the planetary project of the Americans. So, were it not for their barely concealed malicious joy and manifest hatred of Russia, Russian "defeatists" could quite well be called on to be responsible for the strategic policy of the future.

In any case, in our society there are those who are ready to cede Russian sovereignty to the global American empire and meanwhile to defend their position distinctly.

The Anti-Imperialist Supporters of Russian Sovereignty

There are two poles in the opposite camp of the sovereigntists, those who are not ready to sacrifice the sovereignty of Russia, which evidently advanced in the priorities of Russian politicians under the presidency of Vladimir Putin. Both of them respond differently to the challenge of empire and propose two corresponding scenarios.

The first pole, recently clearly articulated by the mayor of Moscow, Yuri Luzhkov, in a polemic with the author of these lines on the forum "United Russia" "Strategy-2020," proceeds from the fact that Russia must preserve sovereignty, while remaining a nation state. Apparently, this belief rules among the upper echelons of Putin's elites, who attempt to counteract globalism and the strategic pressure of NATO and the USA in the framework of a continuation of the Yalta status quo. Connected with this is the obsessive idea of supporting the UN and increasing Russian contributions to its financing, as well as many other international steps. We are dealing here with a wish to ignore the geopolitical shifts objectively occurring in the system of international relations after the fall of the USSR and the Warsaw Pact. Similar, too, is the idea of proclaiming Russia a "European country" (Medvedyev, Putin). Here we see the persistent wish "to cast a spell on reality," to wave aside with words, gestures, signs, and ambiguous speeches the unpleasant sharpness of the challenge.

The Americans openly say: we are building a global empire in which it is proposed to all either to recognize it as a fact, to resign themselves and embed themselves into the imperial project, or to blame themselves (what exactly follows in this case is shown by the examples of Iraq, Yugoslavia and Afghanistan; the other countries of the "axis of evil," including Russia, wait their turn). To this, the sovereigntists, striving not to disturb the status quo, respond: it is not at all so, nobody is building an empire, nothing happened, you must not press on us, let us rather be friends and build together a democratic world without double standards, respecting the sovereignty of all governments, while coming to an agreement about disputable cases.

Then the Americans again specify: it will not be now as it was before, inasmuch as we were one of two empires, but now remain the only one. Try to prove the opposite, and then we'll talk. Therefore, stop playing the fool and give up. "We win, you lose, sign here," as Richard Perle proposes to say to Russia.

The supporters of the "phantom limb" of a failed empire respond: we hear nothing of what you say to us. We did not lose the "Cold War." We are simply democrats (hardly peculiar) and are men rather willing to make agreements (we removed bases from Cam Ranh and Lourdes, Americans were admitted into Central Asia after the raid by the Islamists, we helped deliver Milosevic to the Hague Tribunal, and did not protest against the arrest of Karadzic). So why do you treat us like you do?

The American empire builders respond: why do you think that the fulfillment of the injunction of a master must be taken as services rendered to him? What you did on our orders — okay, continue in that spirit and do not slow down. In other words, you lost the game, so give up the keys to the city. Repudiate your sovereignty. Here the fifth column of American collaborators already sings backup from within: repudiate, repudiate, before it's too late. The sovereigntists stop in their tracks from internal contradiction. At some point, something must be brought up as an objection to the builders of empire on an essential level, both from the point of view of ideology and from the point of view of resources — that is, first of ideology, then of resources. Depending on the model of asymmetrical response selected, resources, too, will be found.

It is obvious that in the era of imperial projects and world globalization the idea of Russia as a nation state, a "European country," "civil society," with its own kind of democracy and without any ideology whatsoever or with some weak ersatz-ideology ("sovereign democracy") (where everything is smoothed over to inarticulateness) will not be considered at all by anyone serious. It will not convince and does not mobilize our society, but at the same time it will not calm the American architects of the future.

What is good in this answer is the rejection of the American plan, an appreciably heartfelt "no" said to the American empire and the unipolar world (all of this is present in Putin's Munich address). But what is bad in it is that there is no "yes" behind the "no," no project; commonplaces about rights, a war against corruption, innovation and business are a completely different story. We are asked obsessively to play chess on the Eurasian chessboard. But after a few moves, we move to the logic of checkers, and then, without warning, even to chapaev[10].

What is characteristic for this group of sovereignists is a wary or entirely negative relationship to imperial projects advanced by Russia, about which the mayor of Moscow, Yuri Luzhkov, declared unambiguously: "To say Russia should become an 'empire' is harmful and unacceptable."

The Eurasianist Empire of the Future

Now let us look at the second pole. It increasingly attracts not only traditional Russian and Soviet patriots from the anti-Yeltsin opposition, but also some Russian intellectuals who made an evolution from liberalism to a great-power position (M. Leontyev, V. Tret'yakov, and others). Here we find those who reject de-sovereignization and the global American empire (as do other sovereigntists), but offer an alternative, aggressive ideological and geopolitical project.

Admitting the irreversibility of the changes at the end of the 20th century, not deluded about the end of the Yalta-based world and the long-term uselessness of the UN, and immune to illusions about the real power and willful resoluteness of the Americans to create, even in the long-term, a world government, notwithstanding protests against "international society" (which Washington holds cheap), this pole proposes to build a new empire with its core in Russia as an adequate response to the American challenge. This is the Russian imperial project. But in contrast with the bipolar world or the Russian [*Rossiiskii*] empire, it must be filled in with a new ideological substance.

One empire can only be opposed by numerous empires that can collect their potential into an asymmetric structure, in order in the first stage to stop, disrupt, and stave off the construction of a unipolar

---

10 Chapaev is the game of flicking your checkers pieces to knock your opponent's pieces off the board.

world, and in the next stage, to finalize among several imperial poles the borders of mutual influence in a multi-polar world.

The supporters of the Russian imperial project reason that neither the territorial, nor the political, nor the economic, nor the civilizational potential of the Russian Federation is sufficient for the task. To reach the boundaries of real multi-polarity, Russia must reconstitute its influence in the post-Soviet space, integrating around itself those countries and peoples that are close to it with respect to civilization (in the first place, the countries of the CIS). At the same time it must promote the formation of a united front of all those alternatives to American empire, from the most gentle to the cruelest, that exist today. In this sense, important contacts are not only the Islamic world but also continental Europe, not only China, but also emerging Latin America; and one must not forget about the other countries of Asia and Africa.

In other words, Russia must think and act imperially, as a world power, which has a say in everything, both in the territories adjoining it and in the furthest corners of the planet. This must begin not "later," when Russia "strengthens internally" (under the influence of the USA it will never strengthen itself to a sufficient measure), but "now," inasmuch as both the tempo and the logic of building depend on what we are building. If we want empire, this is one project; if we are trying to save our state, it is a completely different matter. To transform one into the other is not only more expensive and more difficult, but absolutely impossible. It is much easier, as any builder knows, to demolish everything and build anew. The actors of the 1980s and 1990s demolished everything for us. So the very place to build an empire is from the null cycle.

CIS — The Site of the Future Empire

The foundation pit of the empire, its null cycle, will be the integration of the post-Soviet space. All post-Soviet states have only as much sovereignty as the weakness of Moscow in the 1990s and the potential support of Washington granted. In the remaining aspects, they are almost always "failed states." Today NATO, growing bolder from the stupor in which the Kremlin still finds itself after the geopolitical catastrophe of the 1990s, endeavors to make the breakaway of some countries from Russia — Georgia and Ukraine in the first place — irreversible. In the postponement until December 2008 of the question of the reception of Kiev and Tbilisi into NATO we are dealing with time paid for by Old Europe in order that we use it as instructed. But after Tskhinvali all of this has a different significance. Practically, the postponement ended on the 8th of August 2008, after Moscow's decision to introduce troops into Georgia.

If Ukraine and Georgia were to become part of the American empire, which would only strengthen the position of the Atlanticists in Europe itself (as Paris and Berlin rightly calculated, making a friendly geopolitical gesture in Russia's direction), the imperial project for Russia would hermetically blocked (Zbigniew Brzezinski writes openly about this in his book *The Grand Chessboard*). But the site of the future Eurasian empire coincides in outline with the territory of the CIS.

Of course, speaking of the spread of Russian influence in the post-Soviet space, we are not insisting on direct colonization in the old sense. Today's empires rarely resort to like methods (although, as we see with the example of Iraq or Kosovo, they are still employed; consequently, they cannot be discounted entirely). However, in our world there are more delicate and effective network technologies, allowing one to reach analogical results by other means with the use of informational resources, social organizations, confessional groups, and social movements.

In Ukraine, more than half the population, protesting against the entry of the country into NATO, belongs to the Russian Orthodox Church of the Moscow Patriarch and is oriented toward closer ties with Russia. But Kiev's political elite sold out to the American empire. Western Ukraine is strongly attracted to Europe civilizationally. But the East and Kiev are strongly and unambiguously attracted to Russia. Right now a countdown has started to the disruption of the annexation of Ukraine by the Atlantic empire. The time is until December, although the Georgia-Russian conflict makes the situation even more acute.

Russia has a chance and resources. But if there will not be confidence in the historical necessity of building on the expanse of the CIS a site for a new imperial task, then Moscow might miss this opportunity.

Moreover, the decision to adopt an imperial project must automatically also involve intensive work with our friends, the member countries of the Eurasian Economic Society (in the first place, Kazakhstan and Belarus), whose peoples and leaders support integration. While opposing our enemies, it is necessary to draw together more tightly with our friends, closing our eyes to the different kinds of rough edges in our relationships.

Empire After Tskhinvali

After the events of August 2008, the situation in the post-Soviet expanse moved to a new, much more acute phase. The fight for empire and our influence shifted from political-economic and network scenarios to direct, armed conflict. After Moscow responded to the genocide of the South Ossetian people with the introduction of troops into the territory of Georgia and the recognition of the independence of South Ossetia and Abkhazia, we entered a new imperial cycle. This in no case removes the relevance of political-diplomatic methods of work in the territory of the CIS, but it shows that the military-strategic factor remains decisive in certain cases.

When the President of Russia, Dmitri Medvedev, and the members of the Security Council of the Russian Federation adopted the historical and irreversible decision concerning the introduction of Russian troops into Georgia, and later recognized the independence of South Ossetia and Abkhazia, we crossed a forbidden line, which earlier hypnotized the geopolitical consciousness of the Russian leadership. Putin, while President, went to the farthest extremes to strengthen Russia as a state (the operation in Chechnya, his decree about the appointment of governors, and so on). This was in stark contrast to the destructive policies of the Gorbachev-Yeltsin administration, but did not go beyond the borders of the Russian Federation. After Tskhinvali, we burst this hypnosis, clearly recognizing that it is necessary to provide for the security of Russia and her citizens even beyond her borders. Most likely, Moscow would not have made a decision about such steps if not for the impudence of Saakashvili, whose American patrons swore that an armed response by the Russians was entirely out of the question. He believed them and tried to destroy entirely the population of South Ossetia in order to later strike at Abkhazia, but he unexpectedly bumped up against the fact that Russia has gotten out of its paralysis and is acting like an empire, picking itself up off its knees.

If we are to be consistent, after the first defeat of the Georgian forces, we should continue the military operation, occupy Georgia, and bring to power an interim pro-Russian government. After some time, troops could be taken out, but in parallel, there could be created a strong, autonomous government in Samgrelo, Adjara, and the Armenian regions of Javakheti, that is, a political model could be established in Georgia that in the coming decades could not serve as an outpost of the global American empire and hinder our own empire building. Washington's reaction would be very sharp and negative, but the first days of the war showed that Washington will not go beyond blackmail, while Russia has already lost in its relations with the West all that it could lose. There are no other levers to act on Moscow; the Rubicon has been crossed, irreversibly. In the war for Georgia, we entered into a new era: we stepped onto territory that our enemies thought forever taken away from us. Now it is important to hold onto what we acquired.

We should pay special attention to Kiev's position. From the beginning, President Yushchenko acted like a direct and cutthroat enemy of Russia. He not only supported Saakashvili, but also gave military aid to Georgia, including Ukrainian troops, repeatedly tried to block the entry of Russian ships into Sevastopol, and turned off electricity on our naval base. Essentially, Yushchenko waged war against Russia on the side of Tbilisi. This aggravates the situation around Ukraine, which, in Brzezinski's words, is the key to the very possibility of Russia's becoming an empire again. Now, there is no sense in setting hopes on the Franco-German position concerning Kiev's entry into NATO, and the situation with Ukraine can shift into a hot phase at any moment. It cannot be excluded that a battle for Kiev and Eastern Ukraine is on the horizon.

If very recently even the hottest heads among the Russian hawks admitted only an internal conflict in Ukraine and political, economic, and energetic pressure from the side of Russia, today the likelihood of a direct military conflict is not at all unrealistic. During the creation of an empire, one must always pay: both those who help Washington build its global empire and those who want to defend an alternative world order, founded on multi-polarity.

The events of August showed, alas, how fragile and unreliable the framework of friendship is in the post-Soviet space. The rippling effect of Lukashenko in support of Russia's actions in Georgia in the early days, the caution of Astana in the appraisal of the events, the rejection by the allied states of the CSTO to take a definite stance with Russia in a unified front from the first days after the Georgian attack on Tskhinvali — all this shows to what extent we undervalued the imperial perspective in the work with our friends.

Our enemies proved more aggressive, braver, and radical, daring to attack Russia directly with an act of force (the attack on Russian peacemakers in South Ossetia). Our friends proved more passive and cautious than intended. The Russians and first of all our political leadership behaved themselves better than everyone else in this situation.

Before Tskhinvali, Russia's imperial project was virtual; something was done, but, it seemed, even the leaders of the country themselves did not believe that this preparation would ever come to a specific case and decisive steps. But the deed was done, and henceforth the events are irreversible.

After Tskhinvali, the clock of empire ticks with a quickened pace. Many theoretical problems and debates move to the sphere of direct military, political, and geopolitical decisions.

We have entered into a new phase of building empire. Our empire.

Friendly Empire — The Eurasian Axis

For Russia, the imperial project offers an active development of relations with potential partners in accordance with multi-polarity. These are above all the continental powers of the European Union (incidentally, it makes no difference to them whether Russia is a "European" or "non-European" country; it is important to them that it is strong, able to effectively counterbalance the US, and to supply Europe with energy). After the situation in Georgia and the recognition by Moscow of South Ossetia and Abkhazia, this Russian-European dialogue will be extremely complicated, inasmuch as Washington starts exerting all its power to strengthen Euro-Atlantic ties. However, although the likelihood of closer relations with the European pole has essentially been postponed, efforts in this direction should be continued. The Paris-Berlin-Moscow axis today is more spectral than ever — but as we know, great effects are sometimes born from specters.

No less and perhaps even more significant is the strategic tightening of relations with China, a gigantic state also not intent on unconditional capitulation before the American empire. For Beijing, support of the Russian operation in Georgia will be sufficiently problematic, since

China has its own problems with separatists (Tibet, Xinjiang). But we must not forget that in the case of Taiwan, Beijing, on the contrary, aims to act actively and aggressively.

So inasmuch as it is evident today that we cannot rule anymore with the principle of territorial integrity, nor with the principle of the right of nations to self-determination as an abstract category, but must clearly determine in each concrete instance the balance of powers, the interests of world powers, and the fact of military-strategic control over territories, China can calmly support the independence of South Ossetia and Abkhazia, but not support Kosovo, for instance. And it can expect to find in Russia the ability to distinguish in turn the situation in Tibet and Taiwan for China. But if Russia and China begin to act in consolidation, American hegemony will end along with its appropriation of the power to single-handedly define which principle should be adopted in each concrete instance, the principle of territorial integrity or the principle of self-determination. Thus, Russia and China will be able to help one another create their own empires, not at the cost of each other, as is clear, but at the cost of the limitation of the planetary character of the American empire.

Contacts with the Islamic world are exceedingly important right now, especially with Iran, but also with Pakistan, Arabic countries, and the Muslims of the Pacific Ocean region. This is not merely for the support of resources, but also a source of political will (which was so often lacking in the Kremlin before August). Tehran long ago threw down a direct challenge to Washington and pays for this with an international blockade. In this case, Russia is interested in helping Iran break the blockade so that the energy sector is developed and the level of military development increased. Pakistan is feverish, but anti-American feelings there grow daily. In Afghanistan, the US depends on Russia's support and on the forces of the "Northern Alliance" controlled by it. It is clear that in today's conditions this will be reconsidered and Moscow must find new partners in the situation of a direct conflict with the US. Some Islamic movements, just yesterday Russia's former opponents, can become our partners in the new conditions. Politics is a reality where there are no true friends and no true enemies: he who helps us build our empire is a friend. He who opposes us is an enemy. And an enemy, as is clear, is destroyed (if he does not surrender).

Latin America speaks out ever more loudly about its rejection of American control. Besides those countries that find themselves in the avant-garde of this process — Venezuela, Bolivia and Cuba — exceedingly important steps are being taken by countries like Brazil, which disrupted US plans to integrate the Americas economically under the aegis of Washington.

India is trying to go its own way, experiencing a vigorous economic and technological upsurge.

Through their opposition to American hegemony, each of these countries increases the resources of the future Russian (Eurasian) Empire and diverts toward itself Washington's attention and forces. Meanwhile, Moscow, having great diplomatic experience and quite good potential, could well act as the coordinator in the world ensemble of new empires on a global scale. Our country has all the necessary skills and traditions for this.

Eurasianism as an Imperial Ideology

The most important thing for Russia in this imperial project is ideology. There are no empires without an ideology and a clearly recognized mission. It seems that Eurasianism as a political philosophy for the 21st century has become the optimal form of such an empire.

Among all the types of empire, the Eurasian more than any corresponds to the empire built in accordance with a civilizational character. The peoples of the post-Soviet space lived together for centuries and shared fundamental cultural values, different from both European and Asian values. This independent cultural ensemble was formed around Russian culture, the Russian language, and Russian traditions, opened for all other brotherly nations that had built together with Russians both the Russian Empire and the Soviet Union.

The Eurasian civilization is common to Belarussians, Kazakhs, Yakuts, Chechens, Great Russians, Moldovans, Ossetians, and Abkhazians. Many peoples and cultures mixed in Eurasian society, enriching each other. The core of this consists of the Russian basis, but without any kind of reference to domination, exclusiveness, and superiority, without any ethnic bragging. Dostoevsky called the Russian person all-human, underscoring his openness, the universality of his love, and the boundlessness of his kindness.

Historically Russians were always an empire, which means that this experience will not be artificial. The ideological conditions changed from the Orthodox-Monarchic model to the Soviet one, but the will of the people to unite the gigantic expanses of Eurasia culturally and civilizationally remained unchanged.

Eurasianism proposes to synthesize all the previous imperial ideas, from Genghis Khan to Moscow as Third Rome, and to raise on this foundation a common denominator: the formula of an empire-building will. History, culture, the Russian language, a common fate, the peculiarities of their labor psychology, and a similar ethical and religious structure unite the peoples of Northern Eurasia. After all, were not the Europeans able to unite after so many cruel wars? For the citizens of the future Eurasian empire it will be even simpler. The combination of strategic centralism and broad autonomy, as well as self-government, which represents the characteristic sign of empire, will also not have to be created artificially. This was nearly the way it was in the Russian empire and even in part in the USSR. Something similar was preserved in the Russian Federation, where many ethnic groups and local cultures live their lives. The Russian Federation is also a kind of empire, only a miniature, unnatural one, based not on the real cultural habitats of a common civilization but on artificial administrative lines, which meant absolutely nothing in the era of the Soviet

Union, inasmuch as they were conditional divisions for the simplification of territorial-administrative rule and economic organization. In the countries of the CIS, including Russia, in those borders, as they exist, there isn't the slightest historical sense or geopolitical substance. These are absolutely conditional borders, and only those who rule by the principle of "divide and rule" and expect to lay their hands on those countries separately can insist on the inviolability of the borders.

The mission. Over the course of their entire history, Russians lived with a feeling of its implementation. Precisely for that reason they endured historical hardships and deprivations so lightly. Our ancestors clearly recognized that all of this is necessary for the sake of the triumph of the universal idea — saving the world, light, goodness and justice. These are not mere words — they are all paid for with rivers of blood, intolerable labors and great historical accomplishments. We warred not so much for acquisition of material goods, as for assertion of that which we saw as right, true, and good. For that reason, precisely the coming Eurasian empire may on all grounds be called an empire of goodness and light, summoned to act in the final and decisive battle with the American empire of lies, exploitation, moral decomposition, and inequality, "the empire of the spectacle."

Eurasianism as a political philosophy fits more than anything the demands for the construction of the coming [coming-forth] empire. This is an imperial philosophy, an impressive Russian philosophy, directed toward the future [coming-to-be], though also founded on the firm foundation of the past.

CHAPTER 6

Eurasianism (A Political Poem)

Eurasianism as Philosophy (What is Philosophy?)

Eurasianism is, first and foremost, a philosophy. Philosophy is practically everything. One cannot live without it. A person is not always aware of it, but philosophy moves him. If he does not suspect that it does so, philosophy operates with him as with an object; it finds itself outside of him. But someone who actively and consciously adopts a philosophy becomes free from external manipulation, becomes philosophy's carrier. He receives the inner mark of special philosophical merit. Such a man is always visible from afar; an invisible radiance arises in him. The sole thing that makes a man valuable is philosophy, a talent for philosophizing. This is our specific merit, distinguishing us from animals.

Unlike the crowd of wonderful creatures, man can philosophize freely, which manifests his highest merit. Eurasianism is directed to free people, capable of realizing their own nature and taking their own fate into their hands. Without philosophy, Eurasianism is incomplete, even impossible.

The *Narod* is Love

The first principle of the philosophy of Eurasianism is erotic patriotism. According to it, the *narod*[11] appears as an absolute: Eurasian philosophy regards it as the highest value. But the question immediately arises: what is a *narod*? A *narod* is love. That is why we speak of erotic patriotism. It would seem that the application of such a definition to the concept of patriotism and the notion of the *narod* as love is something extraordinary. Let us look, however, at the etymology of the Russian word, *narod*. It means that which was "born-on," "*na-rodilos*," while this is derived from "*rod*," which in a direct sense signifies "*rozhdenie*" (birth), the appearance of a person on earth. Precisely love precedes birth and plays a decisive role in it. Otherwise no person appears. It is easy to understand that at the origins of the *narod* is the mutual attraction of men and women.

The great power of love is that precisely love propels the waves of generations that deliver ever more and more offspring, create families, and carry out the continuation of the kin [*rod*]. The totality of all beings begotten by an act of love forms a *narod*. The very concept "*narod*" is full of this inner, latent power of love. There is no *narod* without love; the *narod* is a product of love, the product of love between men and women, with a passionate desire for one another.

From century to century, from generation to generation, similar situations repeat themselves: men belonging to a *narod* love women, who are also a part of it. Of course, there are sometimes interchanges with other peoples. But as a result the *narod* multiplies: sometimes the same one, sometimes a new one…

---

11 *Narod* means people, in the sense of peoplehood ("the Russian people"), not an aggregate of individuals ("many people think"). Dugin discusses the concept of the *narod* in detail in his book *Ethnosociology*. To avoid the ambiguity of the English word "people," the Russian has been transliterated. In the plural, it is translated as "peoples."

Mankind is a product of the global love of peoples for themselves and for others. Speaking of the *narod*, we do not mean something abstract, but a resilient and concrete erotic reality. We constantly ask ourselves serious questions. About the *narod* and ourselves. About our *narod* and ourselves. How do I relate to it? Where did this *narod* come from? What will its future look like? We must feel it behind our backs, in our blood, in our genes. It is in our interior and around us. After all, we are only the sacred transmitters of the energy of our *narod* into the future.

The *narod* goes. It stands behind us. But it goes through us. It pushes us toward love, toward another generation of Russian Eurasianist people appearing on the earth and carrying this fundamental feeling of love.

The Russian Body

Why is the *narod* the absolute, main, central, first and last concept of Eurasian philosophy? Because, as love, it gives a man everything: his look, his life, his language, his culture. All that we have, from the form of our eyes, ears and skull to our skeletal structure, is formulated by the love of our ancestors; i.e., by the *narod*.

The torrent of ethnosocial [*narodnaya*] love gave us our corporeality. We are only an episode in this ethnosocial body, which precedes us as the collective body of our ancestors, and which, moreover, is present also in the appearance of other Russian people. And when one of us begins to think about another Russian, he feels the matrix of the *narod*, its common corporeality, his belonging to it and his being blended together with others in it. This corporeality is passed on through us to tomorrow. We carry in ourselves the embryos of future Russian corporeality in the same way as the human body, according to the teaching of Orthodox Elders, carries in itself the embryo of the body of the resurrection. This is a vertical, religious perspective. But the fundamental base of Eurasianist philosophy, the basic element and foundational meaning, is precisely the *narod*.

As a common corporeality, it passes itself on into the future and conquers time, history and space. The *narod* gives us a body, and this is the common body, not the concrete, particular Russian body. A particle of it is given to us as a lease, temporarily. Today, we have it; tomorrow we do not. After all, there was a time when we lacked it. We return it again when the fateful devil approaches, or a sudden incident cuts short our life. Then the body is no more. But the *narod* precedes our birth and outlives our death; it always exists. The relativity of our individual body pales before the absolute, eternal, and endless corporeality of the *narod* proper. The *narod* is a global common body and an absolute value.

The Gift of Language

The *narod* gives man language. What would we be saying right now, how would we think and express ourselves to one another, if not for the language that our *narod* passed on to us. The native [*rodnoe*] body, received from the *narod*, is able to give man the energy for thought, and this is firewood for the soul and our consciousness. But for the work of consciousness, for speech, for words we need language. And it, too, is passed on to us by the *narod*. This language, according to Heidegger's observation, is the highest poem.

The simple utterance of a randomly selected Russian word is real magic, a colossal spiritual deed, inasmuch as in what is spoken is heard the whisper and rustle of those fundamental things, those thoughts, those movements of the soul that stand behind us and that come forth after us. His native language imparts to a man a gigantic energy, an intellectual, moral and conceptual style, and leaves an indelible imprint on the human soul. Without language, we are nothing. Our individuality, our existence without language is absolutely empty and uninteresting. What would we be if we could not speak, if this absolute, great, and super-natural Russian language had not been given to us?! We would be merely dumb cattle...but it was handed to us, and the *narod* did this, for which are obliged to it. Our language expresses the intelligible, the beautiful, the true, and the right.

But this is not only a gift: it was given to us on credit, which we must repay. And therefore we must attentively and vigilantly learn to speak the sacred Russian language. This is the significance of the Eurasianist philosophy (it is not by accident that the leader of the first Eurasianists, Prince Trubetskoy, was a linguist), though it loves more than the language alone. This is its cult and sacred reverence, a most attentive attitude toward that which is said in Russian.

To return what we owe to the language means to understand it, to preserve it, to speak in it about the greatness of the *narod*, to compose hymns to it. Whoever does not speak in Russian about the greatness of his *narod* may even lose his language. The freedom of the Russian word is in song and laments about the grandeur and suffering of the Russian principle in the Universe...let other speeches sound in other languages.

A Russian Falls Asleep and Awakens

The *narod* gave us all that we have. From it we received culture, the Russian word, our form of thought, our homes, our land; for that reason, in the philosophy of Eurasianism the *narod* is an absolute category. We must think about this when arising from bed in the morning. Waking up, one should say, "I am a Russian person" This should be said before bed, while praying, brushing teeth, walking, and so on. Falling asleep, one must repeat: "A Russian person is falling asleep." Only this has meaning.

Now he, the Russian person, goes from one Russian condition, wakefulness, into another Russian condition, the Russian condition of sleep. Thus there falls asleep and awakens the Russian itself, the intelligent and corporeal being of the whole immortal and infinite *narod*. This is what it means to "absorb the *narod*." This is not merely to formally declare: "I love my country; I am a patriot." We must find ourselves intoxicated by our own *narod*. "Why?" you will ask. Because this is our *narod*. It is such and therefore we are such. We do not have the right to love ourselves separately. We must love ourselves through love for the entire Russian *narod*, through love of the Russian in ourselves. Only such love ennobles, satisfies and yields fruit; all other loves are sterile acts.

All that we have said of Russians can be said with certain adjustments of other peoples, too. Or rather, let the representatives of these peoples speak, and we will listen to them and nod approvingly. After all, we are thinking here and now of the Russian person, of the Russian *narod*.

The Russian Person as an Absolute

The Russian person is so absolute that we do not understand the point of the existence of other peoples. "If these are not Russians, who are they?" we think frankly. When we see some kind of joyful, wonderful Arab, for instance, who is not averse to drinking, having a hearty laugh, "opening the faucet," we say: "here's a real Russian." It is not even necessary to drink together; it is enough simply to see: "Here is a good man." It is clear that he is a Russian. That's how we understand it and how we understand ourselves, and this understanding does not stem from appearance, although, of course, Russian appearance is a valuable thing. But non-Russian appearance is also a valuable thing, inasmuch as it is also a little Russian. If we see a special squint, a familiar humor, specific, trembling eyelashes, we say with certainty: "Oh, one of ours!" What do you mean ours?! Yes, ours.

The *Narod's* Borders

Where does the *narod* end? One can ask oneself this philosophical question, if one moves away a little from the thought that it is endless and looks at harsh reality in the search for the end of the *narod*. But this is not easy. Everything is displaced by the acute impression that the *narod* is infinite and has no end. Yes indeed, our *narod* is endless; we do not know of the others, and cannot say with certainty...but still, if we quibble over details for a moment: where does the *narod* end? There, where another *narod* begins. Where does love end? There, where another love begins.

We cannot imagine "not-love." There is no world without love. It will not continue for a single second, but will separate and fall apart. It doesn't exist because there will be no energy in it, everything in it will stop instantly. The world is the energy of love. The ancients taught: "Stones love one another. Flowers love one another." Now very much is said of the eroticism of flowers; scholars even measure the sexual activity of plants. It is understandable that animals and humans love one another. But stones? ...Yes, even stones have love. Both the life of stones and the erotic tensions of mineral energies represent a gigantic area. They love differently, which is why we cannot understand this exorbitant, transcendental love. Maybe the stone loves some kind of grass, some kind of plant. The love of a stone for a tree — sycamore, cypress — undoubtedly represents some kind of energy not grasped by us, but wonderful and clearly present in world. And so: where love ends, another love begins. Where does the *narod* end? There, where another *narod* begins. Although, from the point of view of the Russian person, inasmuch as the Russian *narod* is endless, it does not end anywhere.

There are open and closed peoples. The Russian *narod* is open, and our love is open. It does not limit itself to one or another; it chooses everyone. We love — really love. But this means that, with our act of love, Russian love, we surpass the concrete person. But, you will think — the person! One, another, a third... Still, the most important thing is love, it is more important [than the concrete person]. The most important thing is openness, the gigantic energy of the life of the *narod*. Naturally, everything that is engendered by this love lives, being an element of the *narod*: family, kids, and the state, which is created by our *narod* as a kind of armor.

State-Hedgehog[12]

The state, as a matter of fact, is a very rotten thing. It is not created out of a good life. But the trouble is that the *narod* cannot only love all the time, only engage in love in its own inner condition and find itself in its ecstatic space of contemplation. Periodically someone encroaches on it, someone attacks, ambushes. The state is needed for defense against all of this. The point of a real Russian nation state is to brush aside others, as one brushes aside annoying, dirty flies. It must be aggressive externally and firm, in accordance with necessity, like armor. But internally, it is very gentle, in order not to infringe on, not to trouble that process of national spiritual life, erotic life, which constantly and invisibly flows in our *narod*. That is how we understand the state.

The state in itself is a detrimental, evil thing; it is too formal, too cold. In this steel, in these machines, in these cruel instruments of torture there is little that is attractive. We would like to send the state off. It should be bristled up externally — like a hedgehog. Prickly externally; soft (lively, tender, agreeable) internally, like a hedgehog's tummy.

We are unable to understand even ourselves in our greatness.

Thus, the first and most important point of the philosophy of Eurasianism: the *narod* is absolute. For that reason, when you are asked what Eurasianism is, you calmly say: "it is absolute love for one's *narod*, love for love, an appreciation of the *narod* as the highest value.

---

12 *Gosurdarstvo* is the Russian word used to translate the title of Plato's *Republic*, the Greek name for which, *Politeia*, plays a technical role in Dugin's theory of international relations. It is also used in Russian to mean "state" more narrowly, and Dugin sometimes uses it in that narrow sense: a state is a kind of *Politeia*, for Dugin, but not all *Politeiae* are states (some are empires, some are a *polis*).

There is nothing higher than our *narod*." Others we do not know. We confuse them all. We are unable to understand and clearly identify others. There are other peoples that are able to understand others, but we are not able to. We are not even able to understand ourselves. We are simply a *narod*, and that's all.

The Spirit of the Earth

The second important point of the philosophy of Eurasianism is the concept of the spirit of the Earth, the living space and the world soul. In Eurasianism, territorial space[13] is taken as an absolutely living reality. Space is not an abstract category, but a concrete slice of the living world. In a space there are mineral, vegetable and animal individuals; all of them are its elements. In other words, we take space as filled, never empty. Our space always teems with life and determines it. It speaks through this life about itself and allows one to know it. That's why it vibrates. This is the spirit of the Earth, of our Earth, speaking, which belongs to us, and in which our *narod* moves in time, in a horizontal, extended state, like mercury.

Territorial Space as a Form of Life

A living relation to space, as to life, forms the essence of Eurasianism. We interpret space as a form of life. In his time, the founder of geopolitics Friedrich Ratzel wrote a book, *The State as the Form of Life* [*Staat als Lebensform*]. Since space is the form of life, it cannot be frozen. It resists artificial borders, since it is not possible once and for all to measure it definitely. We are not the ones who build something where we please that supposedly will remain there. All that is needed is built by itself in the right way in the place where it must appear, just as flowers grow or gigantic thousand-year-old rocks lie for ages. After all, they do not merely grow and lie for no reason; they live here. They

---

13 *Prostranstvo*. "Space," also translated as "territorial space." Corresponds to the German *"Raum,"* as in Carl Schmitt's *"Grossraum."*

know what they are doing; their life is in this concrete place, this concrete point of the predetermined Russian space. This is a philosophy of location, of the "place of development," as Petr Savitsky used to say. This is the voice of the spirit of the native earth, which speaks through all beings — crawling, stirring, flying, climbing, falling, or lying about drunk. The voice is directed toward itself, affirming a certain great truth of vital, spatial forms.

Space is a wise phenomenon. In it, in the earth, reason is contained. This reason speaks and shouts about itself, and it is necessary to be very attentive in order to hear it. When we speak of space we usually express ourselves in this manner: "This is my space, that is your space; this space belongs to my country; that, to yours." But we relate to space as to a living organism. Moreover, "mine" is not a sign of possession, but a sign of kinship [*rodstvo*]. Kindred bonds connect a man with the ground, with the living space. Thus, mother-earth. Country-fatherland.

Living Borders

In the Eurasian worldview, the concept of "living borders" is important. There are borders where one living being is conditionally separate from another. But one cannot draw a border on a living being. One cannot separate three-fourths of a rabbit and four-fifths of a squirrel and make a country out of them or build a state out of them. These three-fourths of a rabbit and four-fifths of a squirrel are not a state.

A state and its borders are also a project of the spirit of the world. But if we artificially cut some accidental elements out of these beings, these living spatial unities, and say: "There, now this will be a state; we'll call it Ukraine," we will transgress against the laws of life. Pardon me, what Ukraine? Ukraine in its contemporary borders simply cannot exist, because there are, as a minimum, four living beings from which it took fragments — three fourths of a rabbit, half of a viper, one-fourth of a squirrel, and so on.... For instance, Little Russia is both narrower and broader than Ukraine. In Ukraine there are also a few big geopolitical enclaves: Galicia, Volyn, Crimea, and Novorossiya, a part of which is within the borders of the Russian Federation. This is a very important point!

We must consider spaces according to their inner nature, and not according to a transient, ephemeral state of affairs. For that reason, we, Eurasianists, cannot speak of the "Russian Federation"; there is no such federation, no such state. This is an artificial, ephemeral thing. This, too, is three-fourths rabbit, four-fifths beetle, one stone and an armful of branches. And this cannot actually be a living reality.

The Russian Empire and the Soviet Union were living realities. Both one and the other are mighty, higher forms of life. Likely something was tacked on superfluously with the final touches and something else was not taken in the proper amount. But these were living unities all the same. What we have after the collapse of the Soviet Union is not a living thing, it is a spatial simulacrum, and it will die. Cut a few legs off a squirrel and see what it will do. It will be unable to get nuts for itself and will perish, as the entire post-Soviet state model will perish. Before dividing territories, it is necessary to ask these territories: "Do you lands, you rivers, you bays, you forests, you swamps, do you want to enter into fallow Ukraine, or not?" A referendum must be organized not among dim-witted TV viewers, who are just absurd and historically irresponsible. One must ask the elements, one must ask the mountains, the waters, the rains. And let them vote. One must think, what form of referendum will the elements propose in order that they might express their opinions about fundamental questions.

The Serbian Mountain

If we attentively and lovingly relate to our space and understand its voice, if we learn to decipher its sounds, we will hear what even the mountains say. In 1992 in Serbia I once met a brigade of Serbs, whom everyone had betrayed until that time. When we stopped, we asked them:

— Where are you going and why?

— We're going to take this mountain.

— What do you need this mountain for? There's nothing there, or is it a strategically important point?

— No no, strategically it is not at all important, there's absolutely nothing there, neither water, nor electricity. But this is our Serbian mountain. "This mountain does not want to belong to Croatia; this mountain wants to stay in Serbia. It calls us." Yes, there are numerous Croatian brigades there, and Bosnian-Muslims on the right. And we will go right now, and we will die there.

Why were they travelling there? One might think that they are dummies, completely ridiculous people. What, don't they understand that it is good to live, that they can eat, sleep, stroll, read, and swat flies? But they go and invest their own life in a mountain, because the mountain called them. It said to them: "Men, come here, come. I need your deaths. Your warm Serbian blood must besprinkle my slopes." The mountain spoke to them, and they understood that it calls them. And this is not madness. It is right.

Nobody needed the mountain, but the mountain was Serbian. This is understandable to all Serbs. They are a very lively, fine Eurasian people. That is why Serbs understand everything right away. They say: "This mountain is a part of our collective, this is our friend; they insult her, and we come to her rescue."

Thus, the second element of Eurasian philosophy is the spirit of the Earth, belief in the spirit of the Earth, reverence for the spirit of the Earth, dialogue with the spirit of the Earth, the worship of the spirit of the Earth.

Eternity in Your Palms

The third principle of Eurasian philosophy is called "Eternity in your palms," or "the embrace of emptiness." The problem is that we are strongly, too strongly, tethered to time, to "now," "later," "heretofore," "earlier..." In fact, these realities, of course, exist; thought and formal logic are built on them. But both they and the concept of "time" distract us from the most important thing. At first we think: "We're still young, it's still early." Later we are already adults and are no longer young, though not old, either. Then: "We are already old, not young, and already no longer adults, but pensioners for good." But all of this is an illusion, because through such temporary forms we lose contact with real being. Time is a snare and attempts to fool us, to lead us away from the heart of the matter. Time covers up the voice of being; the call that sounds in eternity.

There is No Time

Some people think that time exists and eternity does not. But in fact, everything is the other way around. Eurasianism affirms that eternity exists, and time does not. Everything that the Eurasian speaks of is the absolute truth, and this must be accepted without all kinds of critical reflections; accepted and repeated. Time is an illusion, only eternity has being. And for that reason the intuition of eternity, the breath of eternity, thought in the categories of space and synchronicity, and the experience of eternity are the main substance of Eurasianist consciousness. But if the eternal is, if that eternal can be an object of our experience, it, accordingly, is here now, too, and it must be the object of our experience.

For the Absolute Against the Relative

Here a general principle is born: "We are the supporters of the Absolute, and we are against the relative." In fact, of course, the relative exists somewhere. Of course, even time has a chance and has its little voice. But this is a very insignificant category and these are very minor rights. On the contrary, the rights of the Absolute, the rights of eternity, and the cult of eternity must be at the center of our consciousness, and everything else on the periphery. But eternity is never substantial in the same way as substantial objects in time. Eternity in some sense scares us because it cancels us out. It removes us, burns us; hence the expression, "the embrace of emptiness." "A philosopher embracing emptiness" is the title of one Chinese alchemical tract. It conveys very precisely the sense of the experience of eternity. But if we shall learn to manipulate eternity, living will be very easy for us; living and accomplishing incredible exploits, making mind-blowing careers, simply delighting in life or wandering around the world and looking around, but only as Eurasians — especially looking around.

Then everything will be completely different than it is for those people who find themselves inside the black car of relativity. Eternity is granted to us, Russian people; it is given to us, offered to us, even bound to us. And whether we want it or not, we must seize it.

It is impossible to seize it, impossible to straddle it, impossible to make it a tool, but there is nothing simpler than to accomplish this.

Those are the three main philosophical principles, the three foundations of Eurasian thought, which are embodied in four supplementary theses. But these three foundations are the most important.

The Absolute Motherland

The three main principles of Eurasianism, laid out above, are embodied in the fourth principle, in Russia, which is the absolute motherland. Russia is the receptacle of the Eurasian revelation, the Eurasian spirit, Eurasian life, Eurasian flesh. Russia by itself is a *narod*, hence the concept "Russian" [*Russkii*]. The first principle of Eurasian philosophy is that the *narod* is love; our patriotism is "erotic patriotism." Russia is a space, it is our territory, and here the spirit of the Earth is incarnated; this is the second principle of the philosophy of Eurasianism. The third principle: Russia is an eternity. Why Russia is a *narod*, we already said. It is a space because this is a state and a territory. But why is Russia an eternity? Because we can understand the very concept "Russia" only if we transcend time.

Russia is an Ontological Concept

Russia does not exist today. It never existed and will never exist in the present. It is always a construction, an idea, a conception, a certain reality that never belongs to the present, but always is, was, and will be in a certain disembodied but also incarnate quality. Russia was, is, and will be besides us. And the experience of Russia is the experience of contact with a reality that can be and is when we are no longer. Thus, in saying "Russia" and talking about our history and future, even of our present, we unintentionally operate with an eternal category, which stands beyond our individual experience.

The Individualization of Supra-Individual Experience

The task of Eurasianism is to make the experience of contact with extra-individual, supra-individual reality an individual experience. A paradox: to contain eternity in time, to grasp the absolute and to transform within it the legacy of one's own heart.

Russia is the Absolute Motherland, Russia is a doctrine. Russia is an order, Russia is mysticism, Russia is a cult. There must only be this kind of sacred relation to Russia.

Russia is a sacred concept. A non-sacred Russia does not exist. When we say, "Russia," then we pronounce, "the sacred." Everything else sounds otherwise; different words suggest themselves. France, for instance, is a non-sacred concept even for the passionate French patriot. But Russia is sacred. Eurasianism is religious service to Russia.

The Ontological Map of the World (Suhrawardi)

Now let us consider the principle "Europe and Asia on the map of being." Two concepts, "Europe" and "Asia," are linked in Eurasianism. From a philosophical point of view, they can be explained by the example of Iranian philosophy, in the spirit of Suhrawardi's *Ishraqi* school of "Eastern cognition."

In his works, Suhrawardi described a map of the geography of being. We are not talking of physical, but rather metaphysical geography. The East and the West are in this being; there is an ontological Asia and an ontological Europe. Suhrawardi elucidates the meaning of these concepts. What is "ontological Asia," the Asia of being? Asia is the East [*vos-stok*], the place where the sun rises [*vos-khodit*]. This is the source [*is-tok*] of the world, a place of contiguity with eternity. The East is a place where the sources of our intuitions are. In Eurasianism, "Asia" is in the first place an ontological concept, connected with "pure being." This is the house where the sun of existence, the sun of reality, the original, fresh, purified sun rises, just now appearing in the sky. The metaphysical sun is one of the most important, fundamental, energetic sources of the solar Eurasian worldview. That is the "Asian part" of Eurasianism.

The Wellsprings of Western Exile

But what then, on the ontological map of the world, according to Suhrawardi, on the map of being, in this sacred metaphysical geography, is the West? Suhrawardi himself calls it "a country of the wellsprings of exile." This is a place of the exhaustion of being's rays, a pole of entropy, a territory losing inner being and inner substance. Here are worlds of exhaustion, worlds of decadence.

According to Suhrawardi, a person's first task in the matter of his awakening consists in his realization, wherever he might live, that he is in the spiritual West. In his usual state, man is as though in a coffin, in the darkness of death; he is as un-awakened flesh, in full ignorance of the possibilities of his own soul, which is seeking return and awakening. But, having become aware of his catastrophic state, he must tear himself from that darkness of the West and begin his path to the East.

The Journey to the Country of the East

A person's most important task, Suhrawardi says, is the journey to the country of the East from the country of the West. That is, the abandonment of "the cave of exile," "the West's dungeons," the well-springs of exile" and the return to the source/the East [*istok/vostok*].

Combining the metaphysical map of being with a geographical map, we discover that between Europe, where before our eyes civilization enters into ontological dead-ends, ontological holes, and Asia, where the traditional way of life is still preserved, lies Russia. With one of its sides Russia is turned to the West; with the other massive, very broad and powerful part, it is embedded in the East and is a gigantic part of Asia, a part essential to it. In this ontological Russia, there occurs a wonderful transformation of the old into the new. The path to the ontological source lies through Russia. Russia is that very path, the path of new birth, the way to a spiritual return — spiritual, but at the same time physical, historical, political, cultural, intellectual, psychological, and aesthetic.

All of this is indeed the deep understanding of Eurasianism, Eurasianism as ontology, as philosophy, as metaphysics. Eurasianism is not merely a balance of some kind of West with some kind of East; it is not merely their dialogue, as we sometimes say for foreigners; it is not merely equilibrium of poles. The essence of Eurasianism is that it is the path from the West to the East, and it is that path which is implemented in Russia. From the West to the East, and under no circumstances the other way around.

The Integration of the West into Eurasia (Descent into Hell)

The West is the extreme of entropy. We can understand it, but, understanding the West, we understand the structure of the ontological depths. We understand how it is there, at the last boundaries of the world, in pitch darkness, at the borders of existence. This is a very important experience, and, according to Suhrawardi, without having this experience, the experience of utmost exhaustion, we cannot gather the energy for a return. For that reason, knowledge of Europe, the moon goddess, abducted by Zeus, and taken away to the devil knows where in the West — this is very important knowledge, but negative knowledge, general demonology, if you prefer. After all, not only Satanists studied the names of demons; abbots, respectable Catholic theologians, were also interested in this question. They wrote out demonic names, familiarized themselves with them, not of course in order to come into contact with them, but to have an idea of mystical geography and its maps, landscapes, populations, and borders, lying at the farthest reaches of being. So Europe for Eurasianists is an absolutely negative category, which can be known and loved as lost souls in hell are loved, for instance.

There is a story, very popular in Russ, of the descent of the Mother of God into hell, where the Mother of God goes to save people who ended up there. And there is practically no good reason to save them, but the strength of her Love is higher than the logic of justice and punishment. She forgives them in spite of everything. Thus, we can love Europe only like we love the strange and incurable sick, lepers, scoundrels, criminals, scum. We can love her, but this is a special Eurasian love. We are called upon to move the West to the East. Therefore, we the Army of the East, the army of dawning consciousness, which wages its war so that the East fully integrates itself in the West, so that, in fact, the West exists no longer, but only one continuous, absolute East. And only Russia can do this, inasmuch as Russia participates in both of these realities.

The Purple Archangel of Russia

In the writings of Suhrawardi there is an interesting section that tells of the existence of a sacred mountain, called "*Kaf*," on top of which is a secret city, "*Hurqalya*," where the return from the wellsprings of

Western exile to the country of the East occurs. An angel with very odd wings stands on top of this mountain. One of his wings is dark; the other is light. This is an atypical angel. He is also called "The Purple Archangel," since the mix of pure light and blazing darkness produces purple.

The reality of "The Purple Archangel" is the reality of the move from Western exile to the Eastern dawn, to the true dawn of Great and Sacred Asia, which is the secret angel, the secret substance of Russia, her historical, spiritual mission, spread over everything — politics, culture, sociology, our history.

Spiritual Teaching: The Call to Repentance

The Eurasian doctrine is in the first place a spiritual doctrine. In a sense it is a prophetic school. It is a point of confluence of great streams of thought, a perfectly self-sufficient doctrine that gives people everything: a meaning of life, energy for creation, and the correct orientation to love.

Eurasianism is thought with the help of the heart; it is the depths of heart-based thinking. Eurasianism is an invitation to the prophetic experience. Let us remember who the biblical prophets were. They strengthened the identity of their *narod*, saying: "Awaken, Israel; awaken, *narod*. You've fallen completely; you've completely degenerated; that is not permitted. How long can you give yourself up to your occupations? Return to your own being."

Do not we, Eurasianists, say the same thing? We call out: "O, *narod*; O, Russian; O, Eurasian peoples, what are you doing? You've turned into such pigs! That is enough. It is time to put an end to the fall. Russia, arise!" We are doing what the prophets did: we are returning our *narod* to our own identity.

Eurasian Truth

What else were the prophets engaged in? They lashed out at the shortcomings of the existing system and spoke the truth, and for this they were often not loved. Eurasianists, too, are not loved much, because when we see where something is bad, we affirm that it is bad, and if we see that it is good, we say that it is good. But most people and the authorities do not like this. They want us either to be silent or to say only good things, like those that are said of the dead. But we speak rightly about everything, honestly and inflexibly, and when we see things that we despise, that are repulsive to our spirit, that go against us, we speak our inflexible words and pronounce our severe epithets. Thus, in certain situations we can suffer persecution. In order to affirm the truth, one must always be ready to be persecuted.

But this is not always inevitable. Sometimes prophets were fed and accepted, fascinated others, and were carried on their hands. Sometimes they were stoned. Both one and the other are included in the prophetic existence. Therefore, if we are conscious Eurasianists, we must bear everything calmly. This does not mean that we must look only for that for which we would be spit on and shot, put in jail and not released... Maybe we too will be fed, celebrated, carried in others' hands, and elsewhere spat on, beat up and mocked. But like prophets, Eurasianists must carry their truth and assert their will.

Eurasian Analysis

What else do prophets do? They restore the connection between reasons and consequences. "Come to your senses, Edom; come to your senses, Sire; you fell away from the worship of the true God, and therefore God punished you, destroyed your walls, your city. Where is the kingdom of Babylon that stood strong? The kingdom of Babylon is no more. Why? Because they rejected the one God." In our time, this function corresponds to political analysis, the depths of political science [*politologia*]. People analyze the reasons for certain phenomena and show how and along what trajectory they lead to concrete consequences. This is an element of Eurasian analysis.

The Eurasian Language

The language of prophets is very peculiar: it is poetic, metaphorical. Eurasianism, too, looks for the category of its language and its analysis sooner in poetry or sublime philosophy than in everyday transient and ephemeral things, budget figures, the names of political ephemera, and empty and fleeting sensations. But our metaphors are so precise, these parables so intelligible, that they are, perhaps, clearer than the most rational, logical explanation.

The Eurasian Forecast

What else do prophets do? They speak of the future: "And I see how a great mountain falls." These are Eurasian forecasts. We, Eurasianists, make forecasts of the future in exactly the same way, in the manner of oracles. We say, "Soon, the foundations of Russia will shake, and evil spirits will threaten to take revenge. Orange locusts will fly over Russia. Dark beasts will lift themselves up from below, formerly constrained for a time by the might of the Soviet Union, the might of Russian statehood. They will lift themselves up, for the times of the advent of this scum will come from all cracks. Our motherland now is not too pure, and here it will be entirely bad."

Eurasian doctrine is spiritual, prophetic. It is at once entirely contemporary in what it addresses and classical in its definitions of those spheres of study that interest the intellectual and political elite.

Eurasian Discipline is the Root of Freedom

Now, let us discuss the last element of Eurasian philosophy. In order to describe ourselves, it is necessary to say who we are not. So far, everything that has been said was so energetic, so deep, so absolute, that, it would seem, it left no place for any kind of opposition, for any kind of evil. It seems that everything that was said is so obvious, so interesting, so correct. There is an abundance of evidence in yourselves for what I said. Look at yourselves, feel yourselves. You are Russian people, you are. You have already been born and have not yet died. This itself is the highest proof of the absolute justice of all the above-mentioned constructions. You are what in the doctrine of Sufism is called *khudzhat*, "proof" of the rightness of the Eurasian idea. There is no need to search out complicated constructions, no need for superfluous and empty discussions. The very fact of the existence of the Russian person is proof of the absolute triumph of Eurasianism. Further, he lives as he can or as he wants, secretly or manifestly, consciously or unconsciously subordinating himself to our Eurasian logic.

The point of Eurasianism is that this totalitarian, absolute, unyielding doctrine, defining you, becomes the root of your freedom. It concurs with your self-will. Truly, Eurasianism turns out to be that moment when you implement the unpleasant command of a leader, exercising your own whim, and when the command coincides with your whim, with your wishes, with the movements of your soul. That is true Eurasianism, when absolute freedom merges into an inseparable synthesis with absolute discipline. In such a condition, undoubtedly, the presentation of the negative disappears and the figure of the enemy recedes into the background. This is fair. After all, in the beginning, to become established as an organization, as a certain power, one must speak of a positive program. All that was said earlier is a positive program. But some attention must be paid also to the negative program. The negative shows itself to us. As soon as you enter the world, you immediately confront the non-Eurasianist element. So how can we conceptually summarize that which is not ours, which is hostile to us?

Atlanticism is Absolute Evil

For the definition of everything hostile to us, we propose the term "Atlanticism." Atlanticists are the horde of carriers of the doctrine of "the wellsprings of the West," the direct antithesis of our Eurasian philosophy.

Atlanticism formally rejects the value of the *narod*; in its place is either the mass or the individual. It rejects the living Earth and the rootedness of people on the Earth, proclaiming so-called "asphalt nomadism." Besides being nomadism (which can also be tied to the native landscape, to the Earth and to spaces) it is also asphaltic, nomadism in an artificial space. A virtual, constant movement along identical McDonalds in Tel-Aviv, Washington, Cuzco, Moscow, Tokyo... One and the same McDonalds, and what, in the devil's name, is the difference, what kind of man chews his hamburger there. There is nothing real in a virtual world. It is asphalt nomadism, ignoring the living Earth. This is the principle of Atlanticism.

MTV—The Personification of the Abomination of Desolation: The Imperative of Relaxation

MTV is an example of classic Atlanticism. The channel is professionally made and transmits the Atlanticist code full-blast, in the first place to youths.

Atlanticism is the negation of eternity, inasmuch as it is founded on the principle of "at least the day is mine," on the base imperatives, "Live now!" "Don't worry!" "Relax!" But in fact this is an order. What do you think, that they gave you an invitation? Nothing of the sort: you received an order. That which you adopt from Eurasianism, and we say this at once, not hiding it, is an order: "Be higher than you are. Be noble, be luminous, be pure, be courageous, give birth to healthy, full-bodied, fine children, make history." This is our order. Yes, this is an order, and we do not hide it. Atlanticists act more basely. They say, "Relax!" but if you do not want to relax, if you are standing, lifting weights, then how should you act: stop lifting weights, or what? And this order, "Don't worry!" "Relax!" if repeated often enters into the subconscious and hypnotizes you. Atlanticism hypnotizes us all. It gives us a brake in one direction and pushes us in another, forcing us to do what we don't want to do.

It might be that Eurasianism also forces us to do what we don't want to do. In general, we don't want anything: man is lazy. But Eurasianism says honestly: "We force you to do what you don't want to do, because we think for you, we take responsibility for you, and you will be better, will be more beautiful, will be happy, even despite your will." "We will make you happy," say Eurasianists, frankly showing people a fist. And they will. But our opponents, Atlanticists, act disingenuously. They say: "Oh well, everything is normal, everything is good. This will do." In fact, they distract us. But what if you suddenly don't want: "good, normal, this will do"? What if suddenly you want, on the contrary, to collect yourself? Suddenly, you want to move down the path of overcoming. But you're told: "Never mind that...safe sex...I thought a little and....that's enough. Let's go have a beer." There's an order here, too, a totalitarian directive. I cannot say that it is worse than ours. It is as totalitarian, oppresses your will in the same degree. Only, we say where we're leading, but they tell you nothing. Because if they were to lay bare the essence of that ideological program, everyone would be horrified, and Russian people would simply destroy that channel.

The Entropic Ontology of the Far West (Behind the Pillars of Hercules)

Atlanticism hates Russia; Atlanticism stands against the East; Atlanticism is the philosophy of the Far West. In its time, ancient civilization erected in Tangiers, at the Straight of Gibraltar, two pillars, where *Nec plus ultra*, which means "nothing further beyond," was inscribed. "No need to go further" was written on these pillars. Whoever who tries to enter will regret it. And while these pillars protected humanity, the gates of the ontological West were sealed, closed by this inscription, by two pillars, and everything was more or less good. Nevertheless, some scumbag still crawled through. And when he passed through that place, he broke the fundamental ontological seal.

Do you know what the dollar sign signifies? It is the two pillars of Hercules, which in old depictions were encircled by a ribbon in the shape of the letter "S" with the subscript "It is forbidden to go beyond these pillars." But on the dollar is written not *Nec plus ultra* but *plus ultra*. "More beyond" is written there, it is permitted, and today the dollar signifies a movement beyond these pillars, into the forbidden zone, to the Far West, to the Atlantic. This signifies that the ocean monster Leviathan, which was kept in check for a long time, has been freed from the ancient networks. And when the ships of Columbus and other European adventurers started in that direction across the Atlantic Ocean, with their ritual gesture they demolished the fetters that held Leviathan, and Leviathan rose in rebellion. This itself is Atlanticism, the philosophy of the Far West, the ontological offensive of the wellsprings of exile. Altanticism is everything that is antithetical to us.

Polarity of Signs

When you see people deny any element of what we are saying, of what we are proclaiming, and even of what we are feeling, know that these are enemies, these are Atlanticists. In a certain sense they know perfectly well what are they doing, whom they are serving, and against whom they are fighting. Therefore, as soon as we acquire the Eurasian mark on our brow, Eurasian radiation around our being, we acquire the aura of Eurasianism. We position ourselves in the world of people rather unambiguously. Of course, this mark can rub away, or you yourselves might remove it, as with a tattoo, but this is not that easy to do. Try to remove a tattoo by scraping it with sandpaper! Nevertheless, when people see you, they consider that mark, and it infuriates many.

So too the Eurasianist can divine the essence of others by their nuances, reservations, external look. Here a man turned his baseball cap backwards, put on wide jeans, and headed out. What does this mean? He is possessed by the spirit of Atlanticism. He serves Leviathan. He sings rap, complacently picks his nose, and relaxes — all is clear. This is Leviathan. Of course, this is not yet full immersion in Leviathan, but it is already, in principle, an object for intent investigation. When our number will be greater, we, undoubtedly, will not let such a character walk through our streets just like that. They'll have to gather in special places, like a ghetto for the sick, and there let down their jeans, present their ugly MTV faces, and jump around on those monstrous boards with wheels. This will be an Atlanticist, Leviathanian ghetto for rappers or skateboarders. The most terrible ghettos will be created for surfers. Surfing is the most impudent, the most anti-Eurasian phenomenon. There is nothing more disgusting than riding with a wide smile on that loathsome board. In one word, Atlanticism is our absolute enemy. There's nothing else to say about this. What's most important has been said. Who has not understood, nothing will help him now. Nothing.

The Problem of the "I"

Now, let us discuss the Eurasian notion of the person. Probably, it is already easy to understand that from our point of view a person is the embodiment of the *narod* and earth. In other words, the person by himself does not exist. He is a conditional fragment of much deeper realities. For that reason, in the framework of one's own people there does not exist such a big dialectical tension between "I" and "You." "I," "You"… if we are Russian people, what's the difference, why differentiate? This is the fundamental question, the notion of our own separation from others, like something indeterminate and conditional. We are determined by our commonality; "person" is almost a conventional name.

Well, fine: today a man is Vasya, but why could he not be Petya? If he is joyous, eats with companions, dances, goes fishing, looks at the sky, participates in political life, writes a dissertation, then why is he properly Vasya? How did he decide that he is Vasya? It is simply that the Russian lives through him, breathes through him. Our notion of the person is not individual. This does not mean that we have no individuality. On the contrary, as soon as we feel ourselves as Russian people — Russian number 15, Russian number 17, Russian number 19 — we will begin for the first time to become aware of our authentic individuality. But this will happen naturally and gradually, not in an artificial manner, nor by the force of false, violent programming. Our own "I" will leap out from us, especially in response to "Russian number 15," and will say: "No, sorry; of course I am not 'Vasya', but neither am I 'Petya'. You called me 'Vasya' and thought that I was 'Vasya'. That was a mistake, a too hurried opinion. I've now become Russian number 15; I'm happy, but I have something of my own, either I had it before or I've just acquired it." And let your soul tell you about that "my own," let it call its authentic name.

We are most often called incorrectly. Before there were special rituals in order to give a child the correct name, consultations with church calendars and with the weather. Other nations have other rituals, inasmuch as the name is important. It is not a minor matter.

A Name is Serious

In Soviet times, parents named children haphazardly. There were Electrons, Vlad-Lenins... parents could even name a child Radio. These are not our true names, of course. Now, naming happens almost accidentally. You were given a certain label, and now you carry it around. "Masha, I'm Masha." Masha?! When we throw off this false name, we become Russians, ordinary Russians, well, or some other healthy *narod*. Then we, through our *narod*, through personlessness, through unification with our *narod*, with our own animated body, with our language, with our culture, will find our own authentic "I." Then we shall say to all: "I am called Macarius; call me Macarius from now on." This will be Macarius as Macarius, indeed. This will be a spark of eternity, not Macarius. But for now it is early. A name must be earned. We have no names. Our individuality must first be created, and if we don't create it that won't be so terrible. There will simply be the Russian person without names, who ate well, and breathed, walked about, lived, and exercised his powers like a Russian with the face of a well-fed man. All the beautiful Russian things will come forward. But if Russian number 15 also acquires the highest, real "I," it is altogether remarkable. We will only say, "Dear one, take this map in your hands, you will be our leader, a foreman or lieutenant in the Eurasian movement." But if not, that's fine, too.

The Heresy of Individualism

Against our Eurasianist doctrine of man as an ethnic being there stands the noxious Atlanticist heresy about the individual. Atlanticism speaks thus: "That is not a man, not a Russian, but simply Vasya. As he was named, so he is. There is only Vasya, only the individual. Belonging to a race, narod, language has no significance. Today he has this language; tomorrow, another; today he lives here; tomorrow, there. But always and in all circumstances he is only an individual. He has a map, a chequebook, a number on his forehead and right hand, a bar code, and a Tax ID Number. That is all. But his nationality, his culture — these are secondary. He is not a part of anything, he is a whole." This concept of man is purely Atlanticist.

Man is Simply a Conditionality

Our concept of man is Eurasian and it is that man is a conditionality, simply a conditionality. And then he can expand the borders of his "I" to limitlessness. For instance, upwards, in order to say: "I am a soul." Or laterally, in order to affirm: "Three or five people live in me. Here's Vasya, here's Peyta, here are two Mashas, maybe someone else, or someone I dragged in here for nothing...." There you have it, a wonderful, broad soul. What a broad life there will be! What an excellent experience. This broadening of human borders and the notion of "the great man" is called "maximal humanism." A man can broaden even downward and proclaim sadly: "What a pig I am!" and he'll also be right. He has a right also to his swinishness.

The Eurasian concept of man affirms that man is the embodiment of his *narod* and a temporary phenomenon, a variable value. Today he is "that" and "thus," tomorrow, a little "different." The day after tomorrow, more "something." But here are constant things: the *narod* and the space; and eternity, which lives through us.

The Imperative of Struggle

Now let us lay bare the Eurasian notion of politics. Our task is to fight and to defeat Atlanticism, to make the values of Eurasianism total and mandatory for all. Precisely this is our program. We begin the path of Eurasian struggle from a position far from triumphant. We have tremendous potential, inasmuch as the country, the space, and the energy of the national [*narodnoy*] soul are Eurasian. But nevertheless our condition right now is far from pristine, so it is very difficult to get through this problem. But it is necessary to raise it. In such a constrained condition, if people will not have a global perspective and a global will, they will accomplish nothing.

Speaking realistically, one must simply fight against Atlanticism, and if we will be able to fight effectively, that is already good. On the whole we must after all strive to completely abolish Atlanticism and Atlanticists. If it works out, excellent. If it does not, at least we will limber up.

We are Going Beyond the Horizon

There are no borders for our actions. So when they say: "But where will you stop?," it is right to respond: "We will not stop anywhere, we will never stop, because Eurasianism is an open philosophy." When we're done with one, we'll move on to the next one. This is a great idea, fitting for Great Russia; this is the Great Eurasian Empire, and we are not planning at all to set her borders. Let others set borders for us, and when bang into them with our foreheads and are told, "Farther, guys, you will not pass," we will endeavor to proceed even farther. And proceed we will! We must live with this thought.

Thus, for Eurasian politics the definition of friends and enemies is very important. It is the simplest thing, but this must always be remembered: we have enemies. Undoubtedly, these are the Atlanticists. We have friends: ourselves and those similar to us. But very many are similar to us, inasmuch as if Eurasianism is understood precisely, it will become clear that we are talking not about some separate movement, some separate philosophy, but about huge nations. We are talking about people, about your ancestors, about your parents. Indeed, Eurasianism is an immense spiritual, aesthetic, philosophical, existential, and political orientation.

Grass Through Asphalt

What is the Eurasian concept of strategy? The strategy of Eurasianism is directed to the implementation of Eurasian principles everywhere, like grass grows through asphalt. It is a very important point that we do not concentrate on the separate, concrete moment. We move in all directions. This is the spherical development of Eurasianism. Thus, if in one place Eurasianism encounters a certain difficulty, it immediately sprouts up in another; that is how plants pierce through the cracks in the asphalt: at first a sprout, then a tree. Then the huge block of rolled asphalt begins to crack, the roots diverge, and the asphalt is no more.

The Eurasian Ark

There is a Eurasianist youth, but there must also be Eurasianist elders, Eurasianist men, Eurasianist grandmothers, Eurasianist bus drivers, Eurasianist police officers — we must have a full assembly of all things Eurasian. If there are the young, there must be the old; if there are the Eurasianist learned, there must be Eurasianist fools; if there are active Eurasianists, there must be passive ones. As in Noah's ark, we must collect everyone by pairs. We must have everyone represented, preferably in duplicate. As in Noah's ark there were representatives of various kinds, in order to throw them on the other side of the Flood, so in Eurasianism there must be directors, actors, soldiers, bankers, bicyclists, people without a specific occupation...

So we must endeavor to find Eurasianists who are representatives of all specimens of society. There are Eurasianists in the President's administration. There are Eurasianists in government. There are big bankers. And there are poor folk who stand on the church porch and beg, who are also Eurasianists.

The Eurasian Network

The further this connection is seen, the better; this connection, which connects one and another, the threads that build up a system of communication between them, a Eurasian system of communication. It becomes clear that all this is not in vain, and that we have been preparing this for a long time and will still be preparing it for some time. But sooner or later it will announce itself in a loud voice. One is occupied with Eurasianism professionally, another episodically. But the main thing is that Eurasianism is the inner substance of the soul, and our task is to create a full-blown Eurasian network.

Of Eurasian Affairs

We must ourselves adopt the Eurasian word and move to the language of Eurasian affairs. Right now is precisely that stage when Eurasianism moves from speculation and from verbal to operative expression. The theory of the Eurasian gesture suggests itself. This is not some kind of finished thing. It is necessary to formulate the Eurasianist gesture, the Eurasian countenance, the Eurasian pastime, Eurasian actions. Somewhere there must be much of the Eurasian *narod* acting together;

elsewhere, just two or three people doing so. The main thing is for the acts to be thought of as Eurasian.

A Simplification of Eurasianism

It is necessary to broaden the target audience through a simplification of the form of the Eurasian message. What we've said is complicated enough. It must still be interpreted, simplified, and tested out on friends and family for simpler ways to say it; the words must be found. These things cannot be designated abstractly. One can work out a simpler form in a laboratory, but it will be somewhat artificial. The simplification must happen through you. It is necessary to understand. And then, the right words, the right terms, the right arguments, the right examples for the slow-witted, will automatically be chosen. This natural process of appealing to the slow-witted will lead to an organic simplification of the Eurasian message.

Eurasianism is a deep energy that is capable of easily entering into contact with other ideologies, ideas, and opinions, simply because it is not an ideology, not an idea, not an opinion, because in comparison with Eurasianism all this is "kindergarten." We speak this way with children when they persistently and attentively bring their fingers to the electrical socket, or threateningly menace mother with scissors. It is at once evident that they've conceived of something wrong. How should we talk to them? Can we right away start reading them a lecture about what 220 volts are, how electrons are running through that place, and that their act will end in carbonization? Clearly, it isn't effective to do that. Usually they are carefully knocked off their aim; they are either distracted or something less dangerous is put in their hands and they are redirected to a different, safer way. We say: "What do you need scissors for? Let me give you a ball." In this moment the confused child does not understand how we snatched away the scissors; he turns in the other direction and is already moving to a different goal, safer and much more appealing, with the ball.

The dialogue between Eurasianists and the representatives of all other ideologies must be just the same, with the exception of the Atlanticists. Atlanticists are our enemies. True, convinced, understanding Atlanticists are rare. Mostly, these are people finding themselves in a temporary state of confusion. We should act toward them accordingly. Give them liquid ammonia; bring them back to their senses. But with people who profess ideas that are not Atlanticist, but somewhat extravagant, for instance, conservatives, communists, or national-bolshevists, that is, with those who recount to us our own ideas incorrectly, we should have a calm conversation, as we do with children who are crawling with scissors where they should not go. "Yes? You think so? Ok." And gradually they must be led into a changed condition.

The Attraction of Allies

Inasmuch as for a Eurasianist everyone except for Atlanticists is an ally, the diversification of discourse is for him the principle question. The Eurasianist must know how to speak different languages. When approaching workers, he begins to speak of the workers' movement, of the fact that oligarchs are bastards, and so on. When he comes to intellectuals, he speaks of the great Russian culture, of Pushkin, of the fact that he erred in certain things, though that that is not important. The main thing is that you must know how to enter into dialogue and through a momentary situation advance the model of your Eurasianist approach. At least, you must show that there are certain fundamental values that you know about and that your interlocutor does not know about, but of which you refrain from speaking in that moment, which is why you are speaking of Pushkin.

Eurasian Strength

Eurasian strength consists in the presentation to society of the resolve to participate in its fate. Its measure is the number of supporters, their quality, information support, readiness for action, coordination of efforts, capacity for autonomous or organic action, and ability to influence the situation. There is a Eurasian organization, a Eurasian philosophy, a mass of Eurasian literature. But the main thing is that there must be a Eurasian intuition, Eurasian brawn, a Eurasian grip, Eurasian teeth, in order to move skillfully in this world full of treacherous traps, perfidious alleys, and dark and unconsecrated entrances where enemies lie in wait for you. The task of Eurasianists is to enter into this historical, fundamental, eschatological game as far as possible.

Eurasian Goals

These are the goals of Eurasianism today:

- To truly become a force; to participate in what is happening with the country; to influence what is happening with the country in the Eurasian tenor;
- To become the mighty leading power of our country; to exercise government functions as instruments for the realization, in concrete existence, of Eurasian ideas;
- To transform Russia into an Empire again; to create on Russia's foundation a very great state, a continental Eurasian Empire, and…
- To participate in the final transfiguration of the world.

Neither more nor less.

PART III
THE RUSSIAN BEHEMOTH

CHAPTER 7

The Structure of Russia's Sociogenesis

The Formula of Russia's Sociogenesis: Constants and Variables

If we examine Russia's specific social character over the entire stretch of its historical path, including all stages and metamorphoses, we can distinguish two sets of criteria. Based on this distinction, a concrete analysis of its substance will become possible. This will help us decipher the meanings of what is happening and allow us to make a more or less reliable forecast about the future.

These criteria can be presented in a sequence of four logical steps, involving both constants and variables.

1. *Ethnoses* (where the Slavic core is a constant; but the non-Slavic ethnic minority is a variable) are gathered into a *narod* (constant),
2. The *narod* (constant) produces a state (variable),
3. The state (variable) becomes a civilization (constant),
4. The civilization (constant) forms a society (variable).

We call this "the formula of Russia's sociogenesis."

And so, we have a set of constants and a set of variables.

We can summarize the logical stages of Russian sociogenesis in two columns of paradigms:

Constants	Variables
Russians [*rossy*] (Slavs)	Ethnic Minorities
Narod	State
Russian Civilization	Society

Clarification of the Constants

The ethnic core is the aggregate of ethnic groups (tribes, tribal alliances, ancestral and neighboring communities, tribal clan structures, etc.) that forms the cultural type of the *narod*; its language, culture, historical character; its tradition.

The *narod* is a historical subject endowed with will and purposefulness. It comprises the root of continuity. Only the presence of the *narod* as a constant makes history possible (in the opposite case, it is not clear with whom that which happens actually happens and what exactly occurs, inasmuch as the significance of a *narod's* history lies in its own deep substance).

The *narod* has a core (the ethnic constant) and periphery (ethnic variables).

The function of the cultural type of the *narod* in dialogue with external and internal differentials (the international context and the inner ethnic variety) gives rise to civilization (an invariable set of fundamental values discernible at every stage of Russian history — in particular, the collective character of social and political anthropology, contemplative thought, the metaphor of the family, messianism, etc.). Its type is Eurasian (both by an external mark, for Russia is geographically between Europe and Asia, and by an internal mark, which is the combination of the European and Asian style in the *narod's* culture).

The constants are interconnected, but are far from identical. There is a definite consistency and dimension between them: the first (the smallest in scale) constant is the ethnic core; the result (the largest in scale) is the civilization; the *narod* lies between them.

The ethnic core gives the original vital impulse to sociogenesis, and this impulse is preserved in all stages of its long-term development. As a constant, this core is permanently present and constantly enlivens the being of the *narod* by its energies. This is evident at a glance in the language and continuity of cultural codes and in part in the phenotype.

The *narod* is the *ethnos* (or group of *ethnoses*) that has stepped into history, become conscious of time, and set itself a task in time. The *narod* is the *ethnos* endowed with a mission. The *ethnos* lives in the present and past. When it becomes a *narod*, the future opens up for it. The *narod* adds to the *ethnos* the structure of an ordered will, transfers the harmonious ethnic being into an unbalanced, historical, active state. In the *narod*, ethnic energy acquires a point of focus, and what was diffuse becomes concentrated in a radial fashion (with a focal orientation).

Civilization is the product of the large-scale embodiment of the well-ordered energies of the *narod* in a developed, universally intelligible, spiritual, material, political, social, and ethical structure. This structure can be regarded as a distinct social code among various peoples and *ethnoses*, which, according to one or another rationale, will be integrated into this civilization. A civilization expresses in itself the universal scale of the *narod*'s mission.

Let us right away agree that the given constants of sociogenesis are not applicable to all societies. They reliably describe the logic and stages of Russian history; in other peoples and cultures the process of sociogenesis can develop differently. This is not a universal rule but a consequence of the inductive, empirical analysis of Russia and Russian society.

Clarification of the Variables

Ethnic minorities are a variable in Russian sociogenesis. Their number, structure, and constitution constantly change. Some arrive, others leave. Yet others want to leave. That is why they are classified as variables. We encounter one ethnic pattern in the first stage of sociogenesis, at the origins of Kievan statehood. Another in the flourishing of Kievan Rus. The third in the period of separate princedoms, *Udel'naya* Rus. The fourth, in the state of the "Golden Horde." The fifth, in Muscovite Rus and, developing in parallel with it, Lithuanian Rus. The sixth, in the Rus of the 17th century. The seventh, in Peter's empire. The eighth, in the 19th century. The ninth, in the USSR. The tenth, right now. Various *ethnoses* figure in each of these pictures. The list of *ethnoses* entering into each of these mosaics would be enormous and the changes in it, great.

Ethnoses transform, cleave, combine, and withdraw; new ones arrive; and, throughout, ethnogenesis revolves around a definite and fixed point, consisting of Eastern Slavs, who also form the ethno-identity of the whole.

The state is the next variable. During a thousand years of Russian history, the state changed its name, ideology, borders, substance, political system, economic system, and legal model more than once. It had different names and corresponded to different realities.

The presence of statehood was constant, the kind of state changed. Each time, the state neglected the *narod* all over again. The narod embodies the presence of state, but not a specific kind of state. The state is a product of alienation from the *narod*. It is a mechanical model, built over an organic whole.

A state is a concrete and formalized system (through right, laws, authority and territory), which represents a set of criteria diverted from the spontaneous popular element. In this, the state resembles civilization. But by contrast with civilization, the state and its transient and temporary orders can be changed and rebuilt through the confluence of historical circumstances or by the will of the *narod*. Civilization, however, is invariable and does not depend on short historical cycles.

Every new state (from Kievan Rus to today's Russian Federation) created by the *narod* (constant) projected ("down" or "backward") onto the *narod* a normative model on the basis of its notions concerning how it wanted to see the model arrangements. This is society (the socium). Society is the product of the projection of a normative social imperative by the state onto the *narod*. Society is always in part popular, [in the ethnosocial sense of "people"] (spontaneously, organically, and in this, constant), in part statist (artificial, mechanical, and in this, variable). At every historical stage of ethnogenesis we are dealing with a different society. This is the reason for labeling society variable.

The variables correspond to the crown of a tree, which changes from season to season. The constant can be likened to the eternally growing roots.

Varieties of States

We enumerated the varieties of ethnic patterns. Another variable, the state form, changed according to the following chain of historical transformations:

Keivan Rus (the arrival of the allogeneic princely elite—the integration of Eastern-Slavic and Finn-Ugrian tribes—the adoption of Christianity, centralization); *Udel'naya* Rus (disintegration in the princedom, decentralization); the Horde (the Tartar elite—the continuation of fragmentation—the gradual rise of Moscow); Lithuanian Rus (Russian-Lithuanian, later the Polish-Lithuanian elite, later the situation of Catholic pressure, in particular the loss of Orthodox and Russian identity); Muscovite Rus (Russian monarchical religious elite—Holy Rus, the Third Rome—the peak of historical self-consciousness); the Petrine Reforms (the German elite—secular Russian Empire—imperialism—colonization); the USSR (mainly of the foreign, often Jewish, Bolshevik elite—the Soviet idea—the export of communism on a planetary scale); the Russian Federation (indistinct post-Soviet elite — the loss of global and regional influence — liberal democracy).

All of these state forms, to which we could add a series of early city-states and Cossack zones ("republics"), have little in common if we compare them with one another formally. Their succession and historicity was secured at the price of the constants lying in another sphere, at the price of the ethnic core, the *narod*, and civilizational factors.

The Consolidated Schema

Let us put this data into a general table.

THE STRUCTURE OF RUSSIA'S SOCIOGENESIS

PERIOD OF RUSSIAN HISTORY	STATE FORM	ELITE	PREDOMINANT STRATA (MASS)	IDEOLOGY (RELIGION)	POLICY	DOMINANT *ETHNOS* IN GOVERNMENT
Kievan Period	Kievan Rus	Grand-Ducal Armed Force, *Zemstzo* Boyars, The Popular Assembly	Free ploughmen	Paganism, Christianity Syncretism	Centralization	Poles and their neighbours.
Udel'naya Rus [The period of separate princedoms]	Eastern-Slavic princedom and city-government	The Prince's Retinue, Popular Assembly	Free ploughmen	Christianity, Syncretism	Fragmentation	
Mongolian-Tartar Period	The Golden Hordes	Mongolian-Tartar elite, Russian Princes	Free ploughmen	Horde Procedure, Orthodox Identity	Submission to the Mongols, adoption of imperial practices	
Lithuanian Rus	Lithuanian, later Polish-Lithuanian princedom	Lithuanian-Russian, Polish-Lithuanian elite	Oppressed peasants, Cossacks	Orthodox identity at the time of Catholic oppression	Resistance to the oppressors, absorption of European-Catholic principles	Poles, Lithuanians

Period of Russian History	State Form	Elite	Predominant Strata (Mass)	Ideology (Religion)	Policy	Dominant *Ethnos* in Government
Muscovite Rus	Muscovite Czardom	Russian Czar, Boyars	The Black Hundred (government) peasants, the beginning of serfdom	Moscow — Third Rome, Russian Orthodoxy, Universal Mission of Russians	Establishment of a Global Orthodox Czardom	Great-Russians
Petrine Russian Empire	Russian Empire	Russian Czar, the growth of a foreign elite	Peasant-serfs	Secularization, Westernization, Modernization	Secular imperialism of the European kind	Great Russians, Little Russians and White Russians
The Soviet Period	USSR	Bolsheviks	The laboring Soviet *narod*	Communism, Marxism, Atheism	The establishment of Socialism, Communism, world revolution	Great Russians, Little Russians, White Russians (the growth of the Turkish factor)
The Contemporary Period	Russian Federation	Bureaucrats and Oligarchs	Fringe urban population groups		Preservation of the status quo	Great Russians

Varieties of Society

The other variable, society, changed in accordance with the following historical chain:

Free Slavic communities with a gradually increasing awareness of their ethnosocial unity made serfs by the princely authority; enserfed Slavic communities, in the process of Christianization and *votserkovleniya* [a rite in the Orthodox church], more and more conscious in relation to their ethnosocial and religious mission; enserfed Slavic communities adopting some Golden Horde social institutions (the organization of society as troops), united by Orthodoxy and nostalgia for lost governmental independence (sovereignty); total society with the prevalence of peasants with a focus on the attractive ideal of universal salvation through a religion and state with stark messianic features; an inflexible class society of the secular kind, devoid of a religious mission, with a clear-cut separation of the social type of the elite and of the social type of the mass of finally enslaved (unfree) peasants (all the way up to differences of language, customs, forms of clothing, etc.); Soviet society, founded on the ideals of equality, internationalism, communist messianism, totalitarian and mobilized; liberal-democratic society, individualized, relaxed, Westernized, devoid of purpose and meaning, oriented towards one's personal career, comfort and material prosperity.

The Political-Economic Forms are Irrelevant

The political-economic forms corresponded to each of the given societies and were an epiphenomenon of the social structure. The state is the center point of politics. It influences the regulation of economic processes to an enormous degree. But part of the political will is concentrated in the society, which is also the main economic actor. Thus, the economic periods of Russian history are a function of the state and social periods, and not something independent. Marxist determinism concerning the change of formations is absolutely inapplicable to

Russian history, and to continue to involve it in historical analysis by inertia is entirely irrelevant and anachronistic (unscientific).

It is necessary to put the sociological approach to history at the forefront and to make it a priority. Only such an approach will allow us to describe Russia's sociogenetic process correctly.

The Russian Axis

Let us turn again to our initial formula of the four logical stages of Russia's sociogenesis. Now that we have determined what we understand by the constants and variables, we can describe it in the following manner.

Three constants form a hierarchical structure, which has a permanent, archetypical character and is relatively atemporal.

Russia's Ethnic Core—the Russian *Narod*—Russian Civilization

We can imagine it as a vertical order, where the vital life pole is located at the bottom, and the rational and conceptual at the top:

Civilization (Ordered Foundation)
|
Narod ↕
|
Ethnic Core (Vital Foundation)

The Russian Axis of Constants

We can call this schema "the Russian axis." The energies of life and culture, the central point of which is the *narod*, circle along this axis.

Civilization and Government

But the *narod* does not give rise to civilization directly (at least in our history). First it creates statehood or a series of state forms, states. Civilization is the common denominator for all these states. They are all components of this civilization and bear its imprint in themselves. We can reflect this in the following schema:

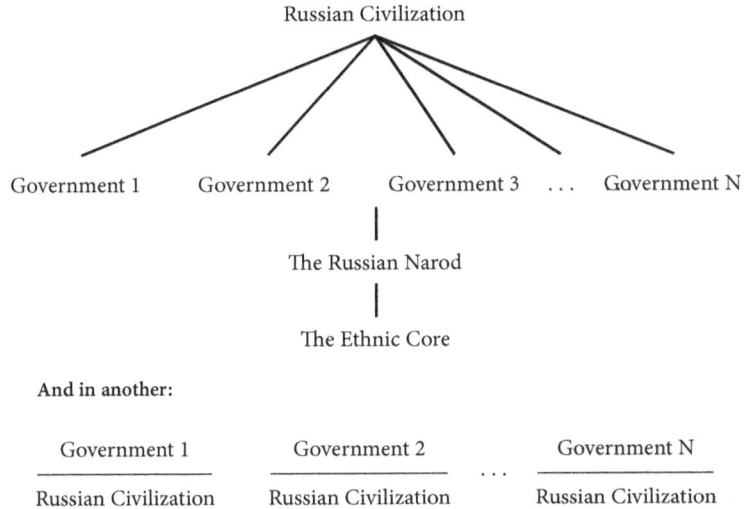

On these schemas, everywhere under "government" one should understand either one or another state, created by the Russian *narod*, or another state in which it found itself by fate's will (for instance, "the Golden Hordes" or the Polish-Lithuanian kingdom).

State conceptually formalizes society. Thus, we can say that to every state that exists in Russian history there corresponds one and the same civilization, manifesting through it in different ways. Sometimes this happens directly (as in Muscovite Rus, especially in the period of the rule of Ivan the Fourth), sometimes indirectly (as in the 18th century or the USSR). In some cases the state can be in direct opposition to this civilization (as, for instance, in the Time of Troubles, or in the epoch of Elizabeth and Anna Ivanovna in the 18th century). In any case, the Russian state always correlated with Russian civilization in one way or another and revealed one or another of its aspects.

The Fraction Society/*Narod*

We have the following picture of the types of societies. This time, the common denominator is the *narod*. It remains constant independently of what type of society is affirmed as a normative in the conditions of one or another state-political regime.

This can be schematically represented as follows:

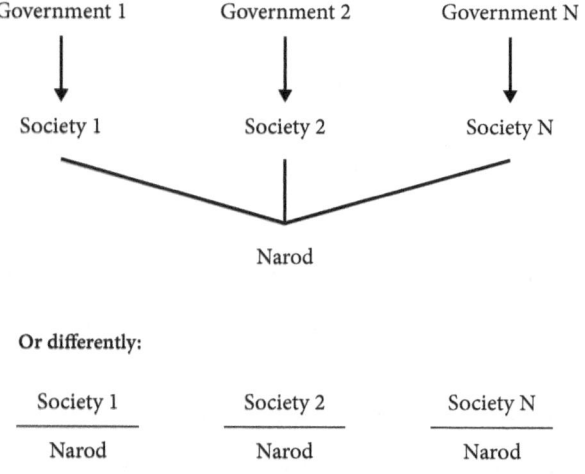

These schemas are exceedingly important for the development of a correct model of Russian sociogenesis. In particular, in the second schema it is obvious at a glance that any historical socium of Russia — both past and present (and with a certain degree of probability, also future ones) — can be considered on two levels: from the side of the numerator and from the denominator of the conditional "fraction" society/*narod*. From the side of the numerator, we will be dealing with a rather rational and logically designed structure, having a state form, a ruling ideology, a juridical and administrative system, an economic structure, and so on; while from the side of the denominator, we will be dealing with a living, spontaneous and volitional authority, persistently guiding social life to the realization of the original mission and reinterpreting this mission through formal social arrangements (sometimes despite them). This is especially apparent in the comparison of the Orthodox-Monarchic model of the Russian Empire of the 19th century with Soviet Russia. Completely contrasting societies (the class-based and classless) existing in the framework of radically different types of state are animated by a common wish; in one case, formulated in terms of Orthodox eschatology and Slavophilic philosophy, in the other, in terms of the Marxist communist utopia. Both societies are fundamentally different in the numerator, and identical in the denominator.

Sociogenesis and the Analysis of Present Russian Society

The model of the sociology of Russian society, described here in its most general traits, has great significance for the historical analysis of the foundational force-lines of the development of Russia and the Russian *narod*. It is even more effective for the concrete description and understanding of processes occurring in the present.

In the current historical stage, before our eyes, there is a new (in Russian history) type of state (the Russian Federation) — of the liberal democratic, contemporary Western kind — and efforts at an artificial construction, from the side of this state, of a new type of society: civil society, liberal, individualistic, hedonistic, egoistic, and consumeristic, corresponding to Western social standards. The state strives to convert the *narod*, with its ethnic components, into a bourgeois nation; that is, into a homogenous mass, united by citizenship, a system of rights, and participation in a common political-economic process.

This kind of statehood and sociality enters into a contradiction with the constants of Russian history, with the narod, its Russian core, with Russian civilization, founded on an incompatible, contrary system of values. In the previous stages of history, attempts to burden the *narod* with a type of society completely contrary to its structure was undertaken only in the period of the Time of Troubles or in the regency of von Biron and ended either with a gradual return to the constant, or with the collapse of statehood and the start of a new cycle.

However, it is impossible to predetermine the duration of the disastrous experiments led by state elites over the *narod*. The Time of Troubles lasted fifteen years (1598-1613), the post-Petrine rule of non-Russified Europeans for nearly forty years (from Elizabeth until the second half of the reign of Ekaterina the Great). The February Revolution held out half a year. The Russian Federation is approaching its second decade.

The Contradiction Between the Constants and the Variables in Today's Russia

We can describe somewhat more broadly the incompatibility of the course of Westernization, liberalization, and modernization of Russian society formally declared by the Russian elite with the set of constants. Naturally, this contradiction touches only the variables (this is clear from the very definition of constant and variable).

Contemporary Russian society and its Constitution are strictly copies of Western models from the point of view of institutions of power and rights, the political system, and economic models. The state variable orients itself on the matrix of another civilization, not Russian and not Eurasian but on the contrary, Western and Atlanticist. Of course, this copy is not absolute, and the codes of Russian civilization continue to work. But meanwhile we must reinterpret the absolutely foreign and external language of political democracy and economic liberalism in the usual intuitive forms. This is clearest of all in relation to the figure of Vladimir Putin. He thinks of himself, in his words, as a "manager," but from a civilizational point of view, he is the "Tsar" and legitimate sovereign ruler.

Ethnic minorities are another variable. In the 1990s, in the period of the fall of the USSR and the formation of the Russian Federation, we were witnesses to how a whole series of *ethnoses* scattered away from Russia and hurried to create their own states. A minority endeavored to repeat this within Russia, which spilled over into a parade of sovereign national Republics within Russia (Tatarstan, Bashkortostan, Komi, Sakha) and a bloody conflict in Chechnya, which we managed to extinguish at the cost of enormous sacrifices. In the era of the *narod's* weakening, some *ethnoses* preferred to maximally dissociate themselves from it (having proved thereby the variable character of their participation in the common history).

Finally, the third variable, contemporary Russian society, is fashioned in accordance with Western models of an abstract, civil society, in no way connected (at least in theory) with ethno-popular roots and ethno-cultural regularities.

It turns out that the existing political regime and set of variables connected with it (state, ethnic mosaic and civil society), stand in direct opposition to the historical constants, which if we take them into account would predict completely different models of state form, ethnic structure, and social organization.

The present analysis brings to light the deep contradiction of contemporary Russia on the level of social structures. This contradiction would have long ago led to an irreparable catastrophe if it had not been balanced by the persistent work of the constants, softening the destructive processes on the level of the variables. This became especially clear under Putin, who defused the situation between the liberal pro-Western elite and the conservative expectations of the masses, partially also *de facto* (but not *de jure*) meeting these expectations after a strictly anti-national, anti-Eurasian, and anti-Russian period of rule by Yeltsin. This gave the whole social system extra stability. But meanwhile, the fundamental contradiction was not removed in any degree.

The current period, accordingly, is a deferred crisis, but we are far from looking to conservatism (the constants) as way out of it. Under President Medvedev, these contradictions started to gradually increase again. Efforts to implement a new wave of liberalism, modernization, and Westernization are leading naturally to a new intensification of the crisis.

"The Party of the Constants" and "The Party of the Variables"

We can say that in contemporary Russian society there are two hypothetical, informal "parties": "the party of the constants" and "the party of the variables."

"The party of the variables" stands on the side of liberal-democratic statehood, civil society, and the introduction of ethnic policies in which the significance of the Great Russian ethnic core would be undervalued and the striving of ethnic minorities to self-determination would be given the green light. An alternative scenario of that same "party," ruling, although in a different way, yet still to the same end, is the creation of a "Russian nation" [*natsiya*] (which historically never existed, and the efforts to create which would lead to a full leveling of *ethnoses*, both the Great Russian and all ethnic minorities). This "party" today dominates in the political elite.

"The party of the constant" is represented weakly and episodically among elites, but it has as its backbone the general population. Here we confront the intuitive sense that Russia is an independent civilization ("Russian" or "Eurasian" as more than 70% of Russians answer confidently, without wavering, to the question formulated precisely in that way by the All-Russian Center for the Study of Public Opinion); that the *narod* has a historical mission, which it must fulfill; that this *narod* rests in its core on the Great Russian *ethnos*, which formed the axial identity — the language, culture, psychological, and spiritual type — but is open to those *ethnoses* that are ready and wish to connect their fate with it and to become part of a single *narod*.

The Putin model of political rule is based on a compromise between the two "parties"; each sees in Putin its representative. The situation changed somewhat with Dmitri Medvedev, inasmuch as his "image" corresponds more closely to that of the classical representative of "the party of the variables."

A Forecast of Russia's Future Social System

Let us briefly formulate our forecast. Theoretically, we can examine three variants of the long-term functionality of Russia as a system.

The first case describes the situation when "the party of the variables" takes power. This signifies that the tendency of liberal-democracy, modernization, civil society, Westernization, economic liberalism, and ethno-separation will prevail over the restrained forces of the Russian constants. In such a situation, the fall of Russian statehood awaits us.

Moving away from the constants, the ruling power will shake the ground beneath its feet and the elites will again, as in the '90s, enter into the phase of provoking a conflict with the masses. In conditions of an economic crisis and the non-decision of a multitude of social problems, but also taking into account the political system of the Russian Federation, it can become a path to political collapse and the break up of the country. In the 1990s, just such a tragedy happened to the USSR, even as the system was more consolidated and answered more to the constants than the liberal-democratic model borrowed from the West.

We should add to this two additional factors: pressure from the USA, by a strategic consideration closely involved in the weakening of Russia, which means that they will expend great efforts on her long-term destabilization; and the very process of globalization, which leads to a planetary spread of the Western model of society and the dismantling of nation states. Advancing along the path of modernization, Russia is moving directly to its own self-destruction (exactly like the "acceleration" of Gorbachev only accelerated the fall of the USSR). Most modern of all (most "contemporary") is the rejection of statehood as such and integration into "united humanity" under the direction of the "world government."

The second variant is that the political system stays as before, but gradually changes its meaning, filling itself more and more with the elements of Russian civilization. We can call this instance the "Russificiation" of the regime. For now, at least during the period of Putin's presidency, events unfolded precisely according to that scenario, giving the system a certain (although also relative) stability. This option suspends all processes in society and conserves it as it is in a half-sick-half-healthy condition.

Finally, the third variant, rather unlikely today, consists theoretically in the victory of the "party of constants" and the construction of a completely different state form rooted in Eurasian civilization and based on the Russian *narod* and those *ethnoses* in solidarity with its fate, as well as the new formulation of its historical mission for the 21st century. This scenario would not guarantee us an easy life, but it would put our contemporaries on one level with our predecessors, who strove over many centuries toward a great goal. They did not strive so that their posterity would repudiate the realization of that goal in the very last moment.

CHAPTER 8
The Russian Leviathan (State Terror)

Fear as Trembling

The German historian of religion and theologian Rudolph Otto, describing the phenomenon of the sacred (the holy, *das Heilige*), underscored that this feeling combines opposite human emotions: admiration, ecstasy, love and horror, trembling, and panic. Moreover, all of this cannot be divided into components: fear cannot be separated from joy and delight.

To the extent that the sacralization of power, the state, politics, and social institutions exists for a *narod*, this complicated complex of strong emotions extends to them, too. We cannot separate out the fear factor as something isolated. Horror before the sacralized political echelon is not separable from love and reverence: consequently, this phenomenon is rather complicated, and to study it correctly, it is necessary to preliminarily describe the structure of the sacred.[14]

Undoubtedly, in Russian history political power and the state were most often taken as something sacred, although in different periods

---

14 Alexander Dugin. *Philosophy of Politics* (Moscow, 2004) (There are a few chapters set aside here for the theme of sacral politics).

this sacrality had a different nature.[15] Thus, fear before the ruling authority was most often a complicated complex of veneration, love, and reverence. Only in a few cases, for instance with the Old Believers and other non-conformist groups, did the structure of fear prove somewhat different, inasmuch as after the schism they regarded the state as "the power of the anti-Christ." In this case, too, there is sacralization, albeit in a negative form.

We will leave holy fear outside our examination here and will focus on a rather simpler phenomenon, on fear as such in the political context, about which Western political science, traditionally operating with desacralized, secular phenomena, usually speaks.

Hobbes and His Monster

Thomas Hobbes, one of the main theoreticians of the modern form of state,[16] expressed the essence of his theory in the metaphorical name of the most important philosophical work on the nature of the state, *Leviathan*.

Leviathan is one of two monsters (a sea-monster, side by side with the land Behemoth) mentioned in the Bible in the book of *Job*, through which Yahweh frightens the despairing, righteous Job, in order to test his love and fidelity. The function of Leviathan in the biblical context is unambiguous: intimidation, the suggestion of terrible and unwarranted horror.

Applying the metaphor of Leviathan to the modern state, Hobbes underscores its main task: to instill fear. Thus, precisely fear lies at the very foundation of the state as a phenomenon and is its central

---

15 Alexander Dugin. *The Evolution of the National Idea of Rus (Russia) in Different Historical Stages*, The Foundations of Eurasianism. (Moscow, 2002).

16 *Gosudarstvo* can mean "state" in the modern sense or "state form" in the broader sense that encompasses the *polis* and empire as state-forms. In Russian, Plato's *Republic* is *Gosudarstvo*.

function. The state is that which inspires fear, and inasmuch as it is a political phenomenon, the fear it inspires is political, too.

Attending to the "Leviathan" quickly brought us to the essence of the problem of political fear.

Developing his theory of statehood, Hobbes proceeded from his peculiar understanding of human nature. From his point of view (shared on the whole by the majority of liberals), man left to himself is an entirely cruel, egoistic, covetous, and aggressive being, inclined to the debasement, repression, and destruction of those similar to him. Hence Hobbes's maxim "*homo homini lupus est*," "man is a wolf to man." If people are not restricted in their natural development, then "the war of all against all" begins. In order not to allow it, Hobbes thinks, the state-Leviathan, is necessary, to instill terror and protect a person from those similar to him and, in the last analysis, from himself.

Thus, the concept of the state is devoid of all sacrality and founded on a wholly pragmatic and rational principle: in order that a man not bring harm to another man and put his behavior in good order, he must be frightened to death. This is the main function of the state.[17] Here we are dealing with an absolutely desacralized fear, a utilitarian fear. This is the fear we are trying to study in Russian political history. That is why we brought into the title of this section the thesis of a "Russian Leviathan." We are interested in political fear in its most utilitarian aspect, from the perspective of conventional Western political science.

---

17 It is interesting that contemporary American neoconservatives, in particular Robert Kagan, are the direct successors of precisely the Hobbesian tradition in their anthropological pessimism. Moreover, in their opinion, the difference between American culture and European culture consists in the fact that the US is founded on Hobbes and his concept of the Leviathan, while Europe is attracted to the utopian constructions of "civil society" in the spirit of Kant, who proceeded from the claim that people's behavior toward one another is usually rational and humane, while egoism and aggression are a deviation from the norm.

"The Russian Behemoth"

In the history of Russian statehood, we should distinguish two phenomena superimposed one on the other: sacral statehood with its characteristic complex of an integral relation horror-love and the proper "Russian Leviathan," an entirely rational thing, called on through fear, suppression, and repression to preserve and strengthen the ruling order. As a concept, "the Russian Leviathan" is an artificial reconstruction, the product of isolating the rational-pragmatic intimidating side of the integral phenomenon of power. As a rational mechanism, "the Russian Leviathan" acts with its repressive might against the concrete social-political lives of people. It yields to rational research and anatomization. The sacral components of statehood evade such a direct examination.

Here a continuation of the symbolic comparison suggests itself. In the Book of Job and in other parts of the Bible, Leviathan comes paired with another monster, Behemoth. Behemoth is a land monster, Leviathan a sea monster. In accordance with the metaphors of geopolitics, Leviathan represents "sea states" like Carthage, Athens, England, and the USA, while Behemoth represents "land states": Sparta, Rome, Germany, Russia. To be sure, the conception of "Leviathan" has different meanings for Hobbes, on one hand, and contemporary geopoliticians, on the other, and this metaphor is used in different ways. But we should pay attention to the fact that Russia, in the classification of geopoliticians, is a land state par excellence, which predetermines its civilizational peculiarities, key parameters, strategic structure, and cultural reference points. This concerns its state forms, too. Thus, the sacral aspect of power, the trembling relationship to it, beyond the dualism of love/horror, can be attributed to precisely the specific character of the state discerned as "Behemoth," in contrast with the rational-mechanical state concept of Western liberal philosophers of politics, such as the Englishman Hobbes, author of *Leviathan*.

Why is there Repression? Four Main Principles

So, against what concretely does the "Russian Leviathan," the state as such, use its repressive apparatus?

We can distinguish various criteria, but we will stop at the four that seem to us most significant and expressive.

1. Dissent, open or secret devotion to a system of opinions, essentially differing from those adopted in the official ideology or opposed to that ideology.

Punitive measures against dissenters are necessary for the "Leviathan" as an instrument for the preservation of stability, continuity, and the reliable functioning of state power. Dissent, nonconformism, always calls into doubt the propriety of the ideological system on which power grounds itself and consequently works as a nourishing environment for a mood opposing that power. Dissent always undermines the foundation of the act of ruling, regardless of what exactly it opposes.

Dissent is defined by the official ideology. That ideology can change; consequently, the criteria of dissent change, too. The foremost goal of repression becomes dissent that has a "revolutionary" character and denies the basic points of the ruling ideology.

In Russian history, the clearest examples of that are the Old Believers and the sectarians (starting from the second half of the 16th century), revolutionary democrats, socialists and *narodniki* in the second half of the 19th and beginning of the 20th centuries, and the dissidents of the Soviet era. Here we also see the clear ideological platform of power, the "Leviathan," and the consequent repudiation of it with the proposal for another alternative on the side of the non-conforming groups of dissenters.

In this situation, "the Russian Leviathan" acted harshly and often mercilessly, using repressive means for the suppression of the internal enemy and the intimidation of the populace, which could theoretically have been filled with sympathy for the enemy and paid attention to his logic.

2. Rebellion, willful reluctance to obey the established order.

This trait is inherent in human psychology and is a constant of Russian political history. A separate person or certain group or category of people, sometimes a whole *ethnos*, at a certain moment realizes the impossibility of long-term existence in the framework of "Leviathan" and displays open subordination. This subordination can be expressed in open revolt, in rebellion, in the capture and looting of the property of the government representatives or privileged classes, and also in the escape from under juridical government into relatively free zones, territories on the outskirts of the country.

We see in the history of Russian rebellions, in the beginnings of the Cossacks, and in the detachments of brigands, "robber bands," vivid manifestations of such a situation, based on self-will and a rejection of the higher authorities.

A rebel differs from a dissident in that he rejects the alienated order of the "Leviathan" itself, the very mechanism of abstracted power, not only its ideological or religious platform. Rebels deny the "Leviathan" as a mechanism of "objective repressions" and the ruling power as the objectivity the right to exist and often propose their own forms of power, justice, and right, founded either on general consensus or on the transparent subjectivity of the concrete personalities of a ring leader, ataman, captain, or chief.

The repressive system among such a collective of rebels can be as cruel or more so as it is in the state, but the principle of the inspiration of fear and the logic of repression is different here in its roots. The "Leviathan" punishes in the name of objective necessity. It inspires fear for the sake of an abstract order, acting as a mechanical function and operating with a persistent fatality independent of all other factors. The "Leviathan" proceeds from the norms of abstract rationality, never coinciding with a separate or group rationality. In this it represents opposition to the will, and the fear inspired by it is radically different from non-state forms of fear.

The injustice of repression is possible in the most diverse situations, but for the "Leviathan" the criteria of injustice or justice are secondary; in provoking fear what is important is the capacity to frighten and execute punishment as a fact. Rebellion is directed precisely against this and not against the injustice of power or the cruelty of frightening repressions. It aims at the "Leviathan" itself as legitimized and rational terror, opposing to it time and again non-legitimate and irrational terror. The rebel strives to reverse the proportions: from an object of fear under the "Leviathan" he becomes the subject of fear, the one who inspires fear.

Like Perseus smiting the Gorgon, Medusa, the rebels place a polished shield between themselves and the ruling power to reflect the wave of fear proceeding from the state and direct it back against it. The rebel group inspires fear among respectable citizens.

This game with the forces of fear can sometimes acquire a political dimension. We see in recent events in Chechnya a clear example of this dialectic. The federal center, compelling the Chechens to remain in the structure of Russia and to submit to its laws, uses the instrument of intimidation. The population of Chechnya takes it in just that way. But additionally the Chechens, by the right of rebels, themselves become symbols inspiring fear, at first as the "mafia," then as "rebels," and later "terrorists." In an analogical manner, in pre-Revolutionary Russia, robbers frightened respectable citizens, as did the Cossack formations.

3. Conspiracy and intrigues to overthrow the sitting Tsar, leader, or political group.

As an integral reality, in the case of conspiracy the "Leviathan" especially does not suffer, inasmuch as most often the mechanism of repression and the structure of rule are preserved in their previous aspect. Consequently, conspiracy does not represent a threat to the entire system, but only to the concrete ruling groups and separate personalities. However, the very possibility of a conspiracy often strongly influences the psychology of the ruler or ruling groups, frightens them, and inspires in them a paranoid complex, a persecution mania that sometimes leads to an extrapolation of fear. The horror of the ruling power before conspiracies gives rise to a wave of repression against conspirators, real or imagined. Thus arises a very important concept for Russian statehood and Russian politics, "treason."

The "Leviathan" is founded on the principle of loyalty and devotion, where systematic and personal factors are intertwined. In fact, the concept of "devotion" is absent from the strict understanding of the "Leviathan," inasmuch as this structure is called upon to embody an impersonal, abstract, rational-mechanical complex. But in practice, especially in the history of the "Russian Leviathan," the theme of the personality of the leader and devotion to him personally is projected from the ground floor of the free, organic hierarchies of the military detachments, Cossack orders, or robber bands to the highest degrees. Thus arises the combination of the ruling power and state as an impersonal mechanism and as an organization based on personal loyalty.

Conspiracy serves as the focal point of the whole structure in this system. In the cold logic of the "Leviathan" there is no place for conspiracy in its pure aspect. It is born when the higher levels of government begin to be identified with a concrete person or group of people. In this case, a real tsunami of paranoid conditions arises, where real conspiracies are mixed up with imagined ones and punitive measures against concrete conspirators grow into large-scale and purposeless terror. We see examples in the era of the second half of the reign of Ivan the Fourth or under Stalin. Subtle is the game at the heart of the "Leviathan." The identification/non-identification of the mechanical nature of government as a repressive apparatus and the strong personality of a leader gives birth to a peculiar form of intimidation, which is projected onto a broad layer of the population, even those that are entirely unable according to their status to participate seriously in "treason." Nevertheless, the factor of "treason," "conspiracies" in their pure form, proves to be one of the intensive moments of the political embodiment of fear.

4. Theft, Economic Crimes.

This phenomenon theoretically weakens the system of government, inasmuch as it undermines its economic logic, its natural orientation to the organization of the spheres of labor and distribution. Theft is entropic and leads to the disappearance without accountability and control of material product created by labor and the partially supporting power of "Leviathan" (through the system of taxes and duties). Different state types react differently to theft. In some cases punitive measures in this sphere are adopted inflexibly and punishment for economic crime is fully comparable to punishment for grave criminal offences, such as, for example, murder.

The peculiarity of the "Russian Leviathan" consists in the fact that theft is most often punished lightly and the fear of the population in this sphere is not too great. From a formal point of view, theft, undoubtedly, is a crime, however it is not a direct challenge to the state. This is the difference of the Russian from Western European, German, or English governments, where economic crimes are thought of as an attempt on the very essence of the state, to which the "Leviathan" responds with harsh repressions. Fear before theft is significantly larger for citizens of the West than for Russians. All the same, above a certain limit theft begins to represent a serious threat to the state, inasmuch as it demobilizes the creative foundation and leads very important material resources away from strict, centralized control. Thieves steal Leviathan's greases.

But here we are speaking of those forms of theft that are carried out by separate citizens not incorporated into the state-bureaucratic system and endeavoring to profit at its expense, as also at the expense of separate particular citizens who earn their wealth by honest labor.

Moreover, the national peculiarity of the "Russian Leviathan" lies in the fact that it itself often acts as the subject of theft, as its own kind of thief, an entropic prism standing between the laboring and the higher ruling authorities and diverting material resources from circulation somewhere off to the side. Theft as a form of the operation of bureaucratic functions is not a characteristic trait of the "Leviathan." Rather, it is a phenomenon similar to the interweaving of personal and mechanical power on a higher level.

In his person, a bureaucrat combines the abstract principle of the Leviathan, the embodiment of impersonal mechanical authority, and the concrete man with his egoistic interests, craftiness, and greed. Sanctioned by "Leviathan," the Russian bureaucrat objects to impersonally serving an impersonal system and theft becomes his favorite form of moderate opposition, the expression of his minor, timid rebellion against the depersonalized machine of government. The bribery, corruption, and theft of bureaucrats are a form of sabotage against the effective activity of the state. That is why this is not at all a simple phenomenon.

The Russian bureaucrat-thief is a national character and, like everything Russian, is ambiguous, with his own peculiar, ironic existential strategy. The personal gestures of the thief demonstrate: I purposely combine the concept of the abstract state mechanism with concrete, personal egoistic interests and thereby in part "humanize" the cold nature of the "Leviathan" monster and bring it closer to the people, inasmuch as through me are expressed if not invariable, then at least fully human traits and not the alienated fatality of the punitive machine. Thus, Russian corruption shows a sort of transference of the concrete bureaucrat-thief from the position of the subject of fear, of him who inspires fear, to the position of the object of intimidation, the one this fear tests (together with common people).

The Proportions of Fear in Various Stages of Russian History

In different periods of Russian history, the state especially intensified its pressure on concrete points, in various combinations and with varying intensity.

Ivan the Terrible brought down the power of repression on "treason". The paranoid style of his rule directed acute fears against "conspirators," against the power of the specific princes and prominent Boyars surrounding him. Mostly, representatives of the elite and ruling classes were punished. Dissent did not really arise during his rule; popular rebellions and disorders were repressed in that regime as before it, and for theft one was punished moderately.

In the era of the Patriarch Nikon and Alexei Mikhailovich and immediately after it, repressions for dissent were in the forefront and oceans of fear were brought down on supporters of the Old Belief. Then and in the following century, Old Believers gave rise to ferment and provided an ideology for a mass of popular disturbances and rebellions from Razin to Pugachev. Theft then flourished as the form of entropy least dangerous and most comprehensible to the ruling authorities.

"The Russian Leviathan" spent the 18th century and first half of the 19th century fighting with rebels and conspirators. From the second half of the 19th century until the October Revolution, the main threat was dissent in the form of revolutionary organizations.

In the 20th century, and especially under Stalin, the "Leviathan" reached its culmination and each of the four foundational expressions of anti-state action was punished in the harshest manner. Stalinism represents the highest archetypal point of Russian statehood, understood as an expression of the "Leviathan": precisely here people were punished mercilessly for dissent (real or imagined), rebellion (or the thought of rebellion), conspiracy (or for the suspicion of conspiracy), and theft (in small and large measures). This was a real celebration of political fear, entirely unprecedented, and "the Russian Leviathan" completely showed its might and its possibilities.

A Digression on The Freedom Loving and Recalcitrant Russian *Narod*

We are often told that the Russian *narod* possesses slavish traits, that it is inclined to encourage repressions and make its peace with arbitrary power. I hold the directly opposite point of view. I am convinced that the Russian *narod* is in its soul as freedom-loving as can be, unruly, absolutely not inclined to discipline, proud, contemplative (if you wish: lazy, sacredly lazy), suffering no higher authority over itself, fascinated by its own mysteriousness, aflame with spiritual beauty, pierced through with a black light, sprouting from the Russian soil, hidden in seclusion from lunar rays and unbending like a spring from sea to sea, from ocean to ocean by its whim, easily, playfully, carefree, fatefully, and festively. This is a *narod* of wind and fire, with the scent of windrow and the piercing sidereal downfall of dark blue nights, a *narod* carrying God in its womb, gentle, like bread and milk, resilient, like the muscular, magical river fish cleansed by sweet waters.

And so, in order that this *narod* does not fall over the edge and does not stop functioning altogether, fascinated by the stars and its own so straight and so white body; so that it does not vaporize in the whirlpool of great insights and does not burn in the glowing skies of a foreign spirit; so that it does not die in the ecstasy of the sweet sleep of metaphysical and abundant idleness; a "Leviathan" was set up for it. They set a monster to trap this *narod* with a red-hot iron, so that Russian life would not seem to him such an exciting, intoxicating drink of honey.

Slavery, complaisance, law-abidingness, respect for power, efficiency, submissiveness, discipline, obedience, in a word, "political fear" — all of this in its native form is alien to the Russian person, who is a monster to himself and therefore fears no one besides himself and still does not even fear himself; he's seen much worse, though in a dream.

"The Russian Leviathan" Today

How do things stand with the "Russian Leviathan" today? Is it strong? Does it inspire that "political fear" that it must inspire?

I am convinced that, despite the lamentation of certain forces in contemporary Russia, "the Russian Leviathan" is moribund in essence. Its body has disintegrated and it has no more strength. It was able to root itself deeply in the collective unconscious: this is the genetic experience of previous epochs and especially the times of the fierce repressions of Stalinism, when its finest hour came. But considering the Russian person's limitless love of freedom, such a mark in the soul and body quickly disappears. The "Leviathan" is overcome; its cycle, completed. Today's ruling power does not inspire any kind of fear in anyone. Only the "ghost of Leviathan" remains, its psychological phantom, the troubled recollection that at a certain time it existed and that it was sufficiently strong, that it oppressed, tore to pieces, ground with its teeth, waved its gigantic limbs around, and did not let go of what was its own. The Russian person looked over his shoulder at it with a whistle and delight. And he looks now, but before his eyes are only the red circles from indecently long New Year's celebrations. The place of "Leviathan" is empty.

Today's Russian statehood is virtual. It is the flat images of a film projector on screen. These are the little springs of an incompletely erased memory and nothing more. Absolutely nothing.

Let's take apart, point-by-point, today's situation in Russia.

Dissent: There is not the slightest sign of repression of dissent, not even a trace. Let's begin from the fact that in Russia today's the ruling power does not have "thoughts" that one could refute. It has no postulates, no distinct ideas, no serious or well thought out programs, no ideology, no political philosophy. All that one could contest in it are technologies. But then there is already a certain entirely degenerate intellectual form of "dissent in the technological sphere" in that. For better or worse, the ruling authorities have performances, which can be considered, but no thoughts and ideas. In this situation, full-fledged ideological non-conformity is simply impossible. Any affirmation, for or against, falls into a bog.

No one raises objections to you, no one agrees with you. "Thought" as such is politely dispatched to the dustbin, or somewhere further. This is precisely the kind of freedom that is categorically not needed for thought itself. Better if it will be burned with red-hot iron, tortured on the rack, or proclaimed in the palace or the pulpit. If nobody pays attention to thought, it becomes impoverished, begins to doubt itself, and pales and fades like a consumptive orphan.

Of course, the "Leviathan" can manage even without all kinds of thoughts, as it does today. But this is not a sign of its strength. More likely, the present situation shows that this is no longer the "Russian Leviathan," but the limb of another, non-Russian "Leviathan." Or the Russian "Leviathan" has crawled off somewhere.

Rebellions and disturbances: Here, indeed, it is still a little frightening. For now it is frightening. Chechens and the supporters of Limonov tried to pull the "Russian Leviathan" by the tail with direct, provocative, impudent, and offensive rebelliousness. What did they not call the monster, how did they not mock him? And a certain reaction was provoked. Its former power was felt. But there is no repressive mobilization, only agony and convulsions. A small, Caucasian *narod*, dumb with astonishment at itself, opposes for almost ten years a regular federal army that beat the life out of the territory with bombs, without differentiating its own from foreign men. A handful of nervous adolescents at the head with an aged writer-pornographer, an "asphalt nomad" of world capitals, arranges systematic bullying; and for years the gallant special services of the army cannot cope with them. Is that really the "Leviathan"? Forgive me, but this is a parody of it. The beast is naked. It has shed its scales. Its claws have been ground off. I am not talking now about whether to cry or to laugh. I am speaking of the actual state of affairs. The ruling power does not yet forgive direct rebellions and scoffing insubordination. But those not "direct" and not "scoffing" it allows.

Conspiracy: There are, were and will always be conspiracies in Russia. They arise with enviable regularity. In the present moment, as you are reading these lines, a group of very dangerous and insidious persons, many of them belonging to the heights of power, plot dangerous and insolent intrigues against Russia and her President. The rustle of muffled voices and ominous shadows intertwine into an obtrusive din in the ears, subtly feeding the nervous paranoia of the rulers. The inner voice does not stop: "Treason! Treason all around!"

Yes, precisely treason, and this is not new. But today conspirators feel themselves so free that the most they are afraid of is a transfer to another post, with a promotion. Those who do not participate in conspiracies simply do not exist politically. Moreover, the closer the conspirators are to the President, the more comfortably and safely they can work their sinister plans. The massive eye of the dragon only blinks.

Theft: This is no longer a theme, but a feast for contemporary Russian political science. When people earlier wrote that, "everyone in Russia steals," that was a metaphor. What "everyone" is can be understood only today. Theft has become the inner substance of the political process. Not a single action is carried out without a "drink" or "kickback," or "betrayal." In contemporary Russia, the aphorism has been transformed into a synonym of "effective politics" or successful "political-technology." Theft is the one thing that constitutes something concrete in our contemporary statehood. The rest is a smoke screen.

The rise of workers' salaries, the lowering of workers' salaries, the adoption of laws, the abolition of laws, raising taxes, lowering taxes — all that happens either must bring "purely concrete" dividends to "concrete" bureaucrats or not a single one of them will be discussed.

"The Russian Leviathan" was always condescending toward theft. But not to such an extent! Soon they'll be rewarding people for it. A medal, "the honorable thief of Russia," is awarded to Pal Palych (to Ivan Ivanovich, Vasily Vasilich) for theft in especially large measure.

The main thing is that it is impossible to blame anyone in this. It is merely that "the Russian Leviathan," honestly speaking, is dying. The fact is obvious. Only the ghost remains, the memory, a certain inarticulate music video.

The resource of "political fear" in Russia is exhausted. As soon as the last shadows disappear, everyone will see that this time the holy throne is empty.

What Should We Do?

The first thing that comes to mind relates to forecasts. So, the cycle of Russian statehood is coming to an end: no big deal, it's nothing, somehow... God only knows the value of this "Leviathan". Moreover, the very concept is borrowed from the Anglo-Saxon culture, foreign to us, from a political context distant from us. However, we do not want to make our peace with this, if we are not morally ready; moreover, before us is not a trade fair of foreign projects, but some kind of dead-end global night, with a tsunami, a worldwide flood and the end of the world.

There Are — There Cannot Fail to Be — Ways Out

One way out is to quickly create a new *Oprichnina*. To compose slapdash from the frenzied service class, driven to despair by the general breakdown, a state organ with stern discipline, quick violence for treason, selfishness and betrayal; with brotherly ideals of the salvation of the country before the coming catastrophe, which, as everyone now understands, was only merely deferred for a while by today's authorities. This is a kind of "Order of the Leviathan," as in the Italian film *The Desert of the Tartars*, where the last privates of a garrison, abandoned by the center, defend a distant and useless border, steadfastly executing their last duty and descending into the night of non-existence with wide open eyes and intense, stern masculine faces.

If this path will be selected, it is necessary to bring into action all the existing mechanisms of "political fear." But inasmuch as fear dissipates before our eyes, we should take up the matter with threefold strength. Quiet Khodorkovsky in a cozy Armani sweater behind an exact lattice scares nobody. If one must frighten, then let one frighten. And here we should not foster illusions. If the ruling power is not ready to move on this real, not juvenile and virtual terror, it is better for them not to venture. Like in 1991, we become historically ashamed from such experiences. You clenched your first: strike. If you cannot strike, stroll along the embankment. I don't know if we have the strength for this. It is clearer to those very potential *Oprichninaks*. One must ask them. One thing is clear: to lift up the "Leviathan" that has been dragged upside down in a puddle of historical helplessness will not be simple. As to Moloch, sacrifices are brought to Leviathan only with fresh blood.

But here is the Eurasian way out: we turn our attention to "Behemoth," to that discarded, sacral synthesis we deliberately did not examine in this essay. There, in the context of the land power, the very concept of the ruling power, and equally so of "political fear," is entirely different. And if we give rise to "Behemoth," then we must re-establish neither the mechanism nor the machine of repression, but the exceedingly subtle and imperceptible sense of the sacred; substance, a theological aim, an eschatological project, the deep and invigorating religious idea that secretly nourished the Russian *narod* in its course through history (as it is said in the Bible about the revelation of God to the prophet Elijah on Mount Horeb: "After the wind an earthquake; but the Lord is not in the earthquake. After the earthquake, a fire; but the Lord is not in the fire. After the fire, the sound of a gentle whisper.")

Russians will respond to this differently, not with indolence, sabotage and indifference, but with enthusiasm for the final battle, the heat of the fiery baptism, the sprint to the last boundary of the national heavens. This is the last resource for mobilization, but it lies not in the domain of technology, but in theology, the philosophy of history, and political philosophy.

CHAPTER 9

Questioning Modernization

Does Russia need modernization? The first reaction: of course it does, how could it do without it? From a certain point of view, such haste in the answer to this question is rather commendable, as is any haste and readiness. But this is so only superficially. We've hardly really thought about what modernization is and about its roots, nature, and varieties. Let's ask this question differently. What kind of modernization does Russia need?

Today, few understand that the term "modernization" consists of two parts. On the one hand, there is technical modernization. More than any other, it is this aspect of modernization that catches the eye. It is embodied in new devices, aircraft, communication technologies, and means for receiving money, in new materials, information technologies, and nanotechnologies. The object of this modernization is to provide instruments and means that simplify a person's life and make the world more comfortable, convenient, fast, effective, and joyful; make it a friendly and user-friendly interface, as computer people say. This interface undoubtedly depends on technical modernization.

But there is also another side of modernization, which historically, as a rule, is intimately connected with the first: moral, cultural, and social modernization. If the object of the first modernization is the development of instruments, in the second case it is the development of the *narod*, society, government, morals, customs, values, and culture. Modernization of this kind has a completely different significance. For instance, the modernization of morals is a rejection of traditional values; at first, a rejection of church marriage, then a rejection of marriage, which is replaced by a kind of civil authority; then the permission of homosexual marriage; and then, entirely logically, the complete abolition of the institution of marriage; and polygamy becomes the social norm.

This is the natural path of the modernization of the family. There is no other modernization of the family. If we want to modernize the institution of the family, we will have to corrupt its traditional norms and adopt new ones. Cultural modernization proceeds along the same path. Traditionally, religious art was the fundamental culture; religious painting, religious literature, religious liturgy. Modernizing this, we came to the period of secular culture, and then to the avant-garde, culminating in all the post-modernist fragments of the world, organized in an accidental manner, which now are also elements of culture.

Moral modernization leads to the disintegration of traditional relations between people. Each person becomes for himself and does not recognize any societal or social norms. Thus, modernization in these spheres signifies a repudiation of conservative foundations, of traditional forms of morality, a traditional worldview, religious norms, the values of the family, the collective, the *narod*, the *ethnos*, the community — that is, everything that constitutes the collective identity of people.

This is modernization, and it coincides with technical modernization. Both are named in accordance with the same attributes: progress, improvement, and development. Under these words, so habitual for us, two rather distinct meanings are contained. The word "modernization" proceeds from the word "modern," that is "contemporary." But that is not merely what happens in our time. The modern is not "contemporary," it is "new." Modernity began when people decided to split from the conservative past, to abandon traditions, when people decided not to look back either to their God-bearing forefathers or to the foundations of their tribes, their *ethnos*, or state, but instead to look forward in the opposite direction. That is when Modernity started. Modernity replaced traditional society. It arrived when people rejected their society's traditional foundations. Modernization starts in this period, from the epoch of the Renaissance in the fourteenth century.

From the seventeenth century, on the threshold of the Enlightenment, the peak of modernization in the Western European world began. In this modernization, both aspects were present: the technological and material, on one hand, and the moral, social, and cultural, on the other. For instance, the manufacture of steam engines is historically, psychologically, ideologically, and culturally closely connected with the period of the struggle against religion, with the marginalization of the positions of the Church in society, and with secularization and the liberation of man from those connections that in traditional society united him with a variety of different institutions, habits, principles, and moral restrictions.

All of this was destroyed by modernization. It corrupted man's conscience, which in traditional societies is centered on the repudiation of one's own identity and the support of those norms contained in the grounds of the tradition, whether in family life or social life. All of this was subjected to derision and destruction. Liberation from this complex revealed new possibilities, which were realized very differently in the technical and moral spheres. In the technical sphere, they are creative, because newer and newer devices are invented. In the moral sphere, everything is reversed and modernization acts destructively. It destroys a man's moral foundations. It destroys the concept of man.

However, even the very idea of man was seriously transformed in the era of the Enlightenment. In traditional society, man was thought of as God's slave. Today people would say that this is savagery, because man is not a slave; he is free. But he was called God's slave because he was free from everything else. He was a slave only of God. Thus, the church gave people full freedom. Moreover, the doctrine that God created man from nothing, and not from God himself, destined man to absolute freedom.

Within the confines of this freedom, a man could choose: should he be a slave of God and master of everything else, of passion and sin, or should he be a slave of sin, the devil's slave, a slave of momentary passions, but remain free from God? This is a moral choice. In traditional society, it was thought that it is right to be God's slave and wrong to be a slave to passion. In the era of modernization, especially in the era of the Enlightenment, it was decided to change this morality. Man is now understood unambiguously as free from God, but not from passion, not from sin, not from the devil. Thus he took his first step to modernization.

Everyone knows Nietzsche's popular formula, "God is dead." However, many do not know how this phrase ends: "you have killed him. You and I." Desiring progress and modernization, people killed God. People paid for the possibility of their own material development and unlimited development in the moral and social spheres with the death of God. This is a very honest and correct view of Nietzsche's, who is not one to deplore or blame someone; he simply calls things by their names. In order for modernized man to appear, it was necessary to remove God from his pedestal. In this lies the godless essence of humanism, about which many philosophers of the 19th and 20th centuries spoke. In the process of modernization the autonomous man appeared and started to call himself "free." Thus, the struggle against God is inevitably an element of modernity.

This is still not the end. When this free, autonomous man appeared, started to spread his peculiar humanistic culture with self-reliance, and completely developed his technological might, social institutions, ungodly liberal-democracy and other discoveries of social-cultural modernization, in that very moment postmodern philosophers denounced Modernity, declaring that man has now become God. But from the point of view of postmodernism, divinized man also creates repressive hierarchies.

And so then there arose the idea of killing man himself. One well-known French philosopher, Bernard-Henri Lévi, proclaimed the death of man. Another philosopher, Roland Barthes, proclaimed the death of the author. Society without people and texts without authors became the norms of contemporary postmodern culture. Thus, man at first killed God, and then, in the search for newer and newer modernization, new liberation, he reached the point that he became a burden to himself. There arose the ideas of the rhizome, the indeterminate half-tuber, the cyborg, and the clone. All of this is the logical outcome of modernization.

This post-human is a necessary element of modernization. After all, postmodernism is what happens after modernization, after modernization has been implemented. In those countries where the cycle of modernity has ended, active post-modernization has begun: industrialization passed, post-industrialization started; modernization passed, post-modernization started. Now they want to drag Russia into this, too. But there is nothing good in this, besides the development of technical means. On one side of the scale are glowing windows, neon lights, TV screens, and household appliances; on the other, the life of man, his fate, his soul, his love, his fear, his air, contact with nature, with his children, and the great historical projects that people set themselves.

In Russian history, we see that modernization never came from below; it was always imposed on us. Here we recall a phrase of Pushkin, who said that in Russia the only European is the government. All modernization comes to us from the West with the help of the forceful introduction of harsh measures. The first and most fundamental stage of modernization happened during the reign of Peter the First, when Russia lost its national character over a whole century. We had foreign morals, clothing, and ideas imposed on us, and for this price some technical modernization was indeed achieved.

The second, more monstrous and at the same time more impressive wave of modernization came in the 20th century when the Bolsheviks started to obliterate everything traditional, conservative, and legitimate, replacing it with their technically blameless experiments, spaceflight, the construction of new houses, nuclear weapons, the disappearance of the village, and the disappearance of believers. Huge successes were attained. Although a little later the communists also suspended their modernization, during the first decade it proceeded in full swing. But later they started to limit it in the sphere of morals, once they understood that humanity could finally disappear through moral modernization.

Technical modernization in the Soviet Union was impressive. No less impressive were the disintegration of morals, the destruction of culture and the social institutions of traditional society, the degradation of the peasants, and repressions. We paid for modernization with many lives. This modernization, too, came from above. A handful of fanatics rose to power and imposed this model of modernization on us.

Of course, the spirit of the people corrected many things and the conservative element made itself known. But we paid not only with blood and not only morally. We paid for modernization with millions of people burned in its furnace, millions frightened to death and left to die. These were the traditional classes of traditional society first and foremost, the peasants, priesthood, and nobility. In order to attain technical successes, the communists had to do what once before them Peter the First had already done when he paved a rotting swamp on the outskirts of Russia with Russian bodies.

Yes, that was an important outpost. From a technical point of view this is very important, but at what price! He destroyed our history, our principles, and our traditions. To people in the 18th century, it was forbidden to walk in Russian clothing or to wear a beard in the cities. Russia paid for modernization with its identity. If we move in this direction again as recklessly, we will lose our identity once and for all.

It is necessary to disenchant the term "modernization." After all, when someone says "modernization," everyone is right away "for it," and he who is "against it" is retrograde, an old-fashioned, archaic, backward man. But we must have the same suspicion toward those people who are unequivocally "for" modernization, inasmuch as modernization is the death of God, and then the death of man, the death of the author, the rhizome, cyborgs, clones, and genetic operations. For now they are still somehow held in check. The EU even proposes to restrict experiments on the human genetic code, as this is a very dangerous thing. But this only speaks to the fact that such experiments are somewhere being performed.

The logic of modernization is that one wants to keep it held in check, but it cannot be held in check, and so-called liberated technique awaits us. People start to look like robots; they're not yet robots, they are ordinary people; but there is a plan to gradually integrate into humans more and more mechanical implants, prosthetic devices, computer processors, and microchips to help their organs work. This is good for invalids, but humanity will not stop at this. Humanity never stopped and acted judiciously. If it enters onto the path of modernization, it travels this path to the end. A person never understands limits; he always passes beyond them, in the good and the evil. His actions will never fall into the golden mean.

Soon our kids will confuse a replica with a living person. Thus, it is very important to separate modernization from that unconditional ecstasy with which we usually greet it. If Russia needs modernization, then it should be of its own kind, a national modernization, taking into account all our conditions. We must distinguish the technical and moral sides of modernization, since in the religious, moral, and cultural aspects modernization is simply destruction and perversion. If we separate these two concepts, that will already be good.

In spite of the fact that it was modernization, our modernization absorbed many national traits, and this interesting phenomenon must be understood: how the Russian element influenced modernization, how it endeavored to deflect it from the direction along which Western civilization proceeded. Here we always had to ask what is more important to us, the affirmation of our identity or development.

From the point of view of Russian archetypes identity is more important, because if we lose our identity there will be no one to modernize or be modernized, since the Western world lost God and fell into the hell of postmodernism. For that reason, there is no price for which we would be able to give away our Russian identity. We must not lose it under any circumstances. In the choice between the Russian and development we must always choose the Russian. If we can submit ourselves to postmodernity, fine! If not, then we must discard it and go our own way.

The question of how to combine identity and development was raised seriously by many thinkers. In *The Clash of Civilizations*, the American political scientist Samuel Huntington advanced the formula "modernization without Westernization." From his point of view, many Asian countries go their own way. Similarly, our modernization must not go the way of the Western world, not to the West, not to Europe. We'll take something from there, throw something else away, but on the whole we don't need it, it is absolutely different and has a different history, a different essence, a different structure, which is why it goes its own peculiar way. It seems to me that it goes to the abyss.

Some are ready to sacrifice technological development for the sake of identity. There are those who think that technology is neutral, although historical experience shows that we must pay with our cultural and spiritual identity for the development of technology. Technical modernization must be separated from cultural modernization. Russia needs its own peculiar modernization, Russian modernization, or modernization with a Russian face. Russia also needs a conservative revolution. This will strengthen us technically and will strengthen our identity, our conservative, eternal principle. Russia must be great or it will be no more.

CHAPTER 10

Interests and Values After Tskhinvali

Revival of the Debate

After the events in Tskhinvali and the Russian-Georgian conflict, a new wave of debate arose in the Western press regarding interests and values. Propaganda operated mostly according to the laws of war and in turn allowed any wording, if only to slander Russia, to demonize our behavior in Georgia and, on the contrary, to present Saakashvili as a victim. However, more honest questions pierced through the torrent of informational wars. Efforts arose to analyze how the Georgia-Ossetia conflict is connected, for instance, to the situation in Yugoslavia or the US invasion of Iraq, to examine and understand what is and is not a precedent. Against the general background of anti-Russian hysteria were heard the first voices calling into question the balance of interests and values. This proved to be the center of the debate. It gained momentum when the intensity of military propaganda, together with its clichés and disinformation aimed at the direct defamation of the opponent, began to abate. The question became this, how does Russian resoluteness in Georgia influence the balance of interests and values?

Interests and Rules

Discussions about the correlation of values and interests in the 21st century took place in the Western European and American press. Everyone accepts the obvious fact that great and regional powers have their own interests. As in the case of the interests of separate groups, companies, or countries, these interests clash with those of other groups and countries. Such is the character of interests: they are by definition egotistic. They often give rise to conflict and lead to an increase in tension.

In fact, this is a peculiarity of human psychology. Everyone strives to broaden the zone of his control at the cost of others. The whole question consists in how to find the formula to legitimately defend your interests while recognizing certain general rules. These rules, their structure and substance, comprise the most essential question in international relations. They are called on to regulate the clash of interests. But these very rules are not pulled out of thin air. They strengthen the actual balance of power, calling on all actors to act within the framework of the status quo.

After the fall of the USSR, these rules started to change radically, in parallel with the change of the spread of forces. The rules of the bipolar word ceded their place to those of the unipolar world created before our eyes, so that the model of regulating conflicts of interest started to take shape all over again, first of all with reference to the US. In this situation, the interests of the US were gradually identified with the "general good" and support for the world order. This shift of the balance of powers brought with it a substantial adjustment of the understanding of what to count as legitimate and illegitimate interests.

American neoconservatives who completely identified American interests with global interests, giving all others only the freedom to align with America's policies and to adapt their own interests to it, expressed themselves more clearly than the rest in this question. In the unipolar model of the world, local and regional interests that, as a minimum, did not contradict the Americans were recognized as legitimate. Everything else was categorized as illegitimate by the right of force and by the fact of victory in the "Cold War," which the Americans and their supporters were certain about.

If earlier the interests of the USSR and the countries of the Warsaw pact, which could be contested only on the "no man's land" of the Third World, were recognized as legitimate, together, partially, with the actions of the non-allied nations, expertly maneuvering between the two poles, now the entire situation has drastically changed and the Americans have completely appropriated to themselves the right of judging about the legality or illegality of interests.

From Interests to Values

In the Western European and American press the idea is voiced more and more recently that values relate to a sphere that in the 21st century must prevail over the domain of interests. As a rule, by "values" here were understood the values of the Western world: human rights, democracy, the free market, liberalism, global security, and ecology. They were announced as "universal." And consequently, they must be adopted and shared by all countries and peoples, including those with strictly opposed interests.

According to this approach, values unite and interests divide. Under the aegis of general values, it was proposed to those who abide by them to waive their own political, economic, strategic, and geopolitical interests. The unconditional values of human life, social development, freedom and democracy, sacred private property, etc., transferred rivalry in the sphere of interests into new forms, where many methods states used for centuries to defend their interests would prove inadmissible. In the first place, there was talk of the restriction of military methods and other forms of violence.

The US Declared Its Interests Universal Values

It was, however, soon discovered that this kindly offer to everyone to be guided in the first place by values, and only later by interests, made many skeptical. It became clear that persuading everyone of their devotion to values, the main arbiter of the unipolar world, the US, in fact cynically realized its own interests. It turned out that the Americans not only made their own national interests the only ones actually legitimate, but also announced them through a universal system of values. In other words, American values were in the first place called universal values, and the interests of the US were raised to a certain universal law. This identification invalidated the whole moral pathos of the discussion of the exercise of values over interests, inasmuch as the Americans themselves were not prepared to set an example by their actions. There was no single instance in which they would put "values" higher than their own interests. On the contrary, they continued to act egotistically and cynically; for instance, by refusing to sign the Kyoto Protocols and other documents concerning ecology.

Rather than saying that America simply wants to control the natural resources in the Middle East and for that reason, proceeding from a strategic consideration, the US occupied Iraq, as would have been understood in the 19th century, when everyone reasoned with the category of interests, not of values, Washington speaks of something entirely different. The Americans cynically refer, officially, to the legally and logically unjustified invasion as a value-phenomenon, referring to "the export of democracy" and the punishment of the "terrorist regime of Saddam Hussein."

Even before the events in Tskhinvali the following circumstance became evident. The Americans called on everyone to follow "universal values" and to waive their interests, but not only did they not adhere to these themselves, on the contrary, the Americans erected their own national egotistical interests as the highest values. This paradox was noticed almost immediately, and many people, whose common sense cannot be changed, took to criticizing this position. This includes the Europeans, too, who told the Americans that if they need to be guided by universal values then everyone together should waive their interests.

Western Values Are Not Universal; Different Peoples Have Other Values

But there is still another consideration. Why, properly speaking, did humanity adopt the values of freedom and democracy, human rights, the market economy, social progress, and technological development as universal? This is a fundamental question, which is practically never posed by the Western press. After all, if we look at the number of people living today on the planet, we will see that the great majority of them hold entirely different values. The market and democracy, for instance, do not emerge from the social and political history of Indian society, where even today the caste system is preserved. There are billions of such people. These values are not at all characteristic of the Chinese tradition, but there are another billion people in China. A billion Muslims have absolutely their own view on what to consider the highest value (here what is most important is fear of God and following of religious instructions, and only then everything else). The same can be said of the peoples of Africa, the East, and for that matter Russia. The values of the market, liberal democracy, and social progress in the sense in which the West gives them, are not at all self-evident for Russian history and Russian society, since in the vast majority of historical stages (as before the Revolution, so after it) Russians held to absolutely different value arrangements.

Values that seem universal to the contemporary European or American are absolutely not so for the contemporary Chinese, Indian, or Russian. They might be attractive or repulsive, but the main thing is that they are not universal. Nothing in the history of the greater part of mankind, excluding the experience of Western countries, testifies that these values grew everywhere independently and were not imposed in a colonial manner, practically by force.

Russia is not a European Country, but a Eurasian Civilization

There are two historical and semantic substitutions: 1) Western European values are presented as universal and 2) under the guise of the defense of these values, Americans are guided by their own interests. It turns out that whole debate about interests and values has a propagandistic character, being an attempt to implant in the consciousness of humanity two absolutely false ideas. The first is that the Western system of values is universal and invariable. When Putin and Medvedev announced that, "Russia is a European country," this was evidence of the fact that they had fallen under the hypnosis of the idea of the universality of Western values. However, Russia is in fact not a European country, but a Eurasian civilization.

Even at the first, still neutral stage, the theme of values bore some veiled racism. Indeed, is it not racism when some one part of humanity, "advanced," "progressive," "civilized," is taken as the standard, and all other historical experiences and socio-political systems are reduced to something "defective," "backward," "barbarian"?

The second substitution is even more cynical. It was declared that universal values are American interests. I'll remind you where the origins of such pretension lie. They are rooted in the doctrine of former US Present Woodrow Wilson, who at the start of the 20th century in the period of the First World War announced that America's main task was the spread of democracy throughout the world. It was postulated that the American state was the optimal model for the development of humanity and thus that the US not only could but must interfere in world politics to establish its own unique principles. Thus, still in the 1920s, the Council on Foreign Relations was created to realize this idea, and in the course of things the idea of the creation of

World Government matured, according to which it was necessary to affirm the American model as the sole model for all and thereby to subordinate other countries and peoples to the American ideological construction. The idea of the identification of the values and interests of the USA with universal values has an almost century long history, over the course of which Americans steadfastly proceeded to the creation of a World Government.

What followed in practice from this debate about values? Countries and peoples, including those of continental Europe whose interests do not coincide entirely with American interests, must recognize the value system of the US and subordinate their interests precisely to those values that are in essence identical with American interests. If we call things by their own names, we have before us simply the idea of direct colonization. This is the affirmation of the correctness and universality of one country, one pole, one hyper-state, where all other states follow in its channels, recognizing that it alone is "the path to salvation," "development," "freedom" and so on. Those who do not agree with this are demonized and written into the black list of "enemies of humanity"; sometimes they are occupied, like Afghanistan or Iraq.

Tskhinvali Put an End to the Debate about Values

All the substitutions and paradoxes of the debate about values and interests were clearly exposed in the events in Tskhinvali. The Georgian leader Saakashvili attacked Russia. He attacked precisely Russia. After all, the Georgian forces shot at our peacekeepers and subjected our citizens to a planned genocide in the person of the elders, women, and children of South Ossetia. Despite this fact, the West and the US pretend that nothing happened and continue to stand for Saakashvili, who supposedly "fights heroically against Russian aggression." According to this model, Saakashvili, on one hand, corresponds to American interests, inasmuch as he offers to locate American military bases in

Georgia, and on the other hand, if we take values into account, acts as a "champion of democracy" against the supposedly "authoritarian Russian regime." The fact that Saakashvili, "good" from the point of view of American values and "advantageous" from the point of view of American interests, acts in the most savage manner and destroys peaceful citizens, dealing a final blow to the backs of the heads of injured peacemakers, does not stop the Americans from standing entirely on his side.

After Russia saves the peoples of South Ossetia and Abkhazia from genocide, firmly and symmetrically responding to direct military challenge, it will recognize their political right to form their own state. Here a question arises: how should we categorize such behavior by Russia from the point of view of values and interests?

In the first place, it is entirely evident that in its reaction to the attack on Tskhinvali, Moscow was guided by precisely universal values. But it turned out that the understanding of these values fundamentally diverges between the West and us. Let us call things by their names: Russia thinks that the value of people's right to life is the highest value, and that if a real genocide is being carried out before our eyes, it must interfere, even more so when we're talking about citizens of the Russian Federation and when the conflict arises on the periphery of our borders. Despite the fact that the US and Western society do not recognize the massacre of Ossetians as genocide and the shooting up of a peaceful city from "Grad" stations with heavy artillery a crime, Russia challenges these double standards. If genocide is not genocide, the murder of peaceful citizens not murder, and crime not crime, then we put entirely under question the existence of universal values, which is what Russia said in August of 2008. If the West, with its morals, has gone so far as to ignore the most obvious things, then, excuse me, but we do not share the same path. In this respect, Russia did not give up on its values.

In South Ossetia and Abkhazia, for the first time in many decades of pro-Western hypnosis, Russia started to act from its personal understanding of what is good, what is bad, what may be done, what may not be done, what is permissible, what impermissible, what impossible, and what criminal. Here we encounter an important reality. Our understanding of what the highest value is (for instance, the human right to life, a people's right to life) ran counter to the completely different view of the US and the West. After all, if we're talking about the right to life of those peoples that were oriented toward Russia and not toward the USA, this right carries no weight, which is why the shelling of Tskhinvali was not a crime.

We Defended Our Values—Hence, We're Right

Values. We parted from the US and the West in the understanding of values. This is a fundamental question. We adequately responded to the violation of that which is for us self-evident, the rights of a people to exist. And here we were as consistent as ever: we recognized the right to life not only of the South Ossetians or Abkhazians, but also of the Albanians, Croats, and Bosnians, as well as of the Serbs, regardless of whether they live in Serbia or in enclaves of other states. Moscow insisted that the Serbs must not be submitted to genocide from the side of the Albanians and Croats, but also that Kosovar Albanians must not be submitted to genocide from the side of the Serbs. Russia judged ethnic cleansings carried out by the Serbs (if any) exactly as it judged ethnic cleansings carried out against the Serbs themselves. We did not defend any value whatsoever, but wanted justice, and therefore rather softly and carefully opposed the US on the question of Yugoslavia. But for their part the Americans did violence to this value system in their own interests.

Thus, after Tskhinvali Russia finally awoke from the hypnosis of a supposedly "universal" system of values. This is an essential point.

In August of 2008, Russia left this chimerical consensus, this hypnotic community of people who share "universal" Western values, in the first place because the West itself started to break up their construction, having clearly emphasized that there is nothing universal in these values, an event the significance of which cannot be overemphasized because it is fraught with large-scale consequences. Henceforth, for Russia there is no united world value-system. In our understanding of what is and what is not a value, what is the highest value and what secondary, we will now rely only on ourselves.

Our society thus rediscovers the treasure of its national traditions, both monarchic and Soviet. Russians, especially conscious Russians, always clearly understood that the values of our society, growing from Orthodox traditions and our domestic history, differed essentially from those of the West. Only in the 1990s was there are attempt to inculcate in us the illusory idea of the universality of the political-economic path, social progress, and technological development, which supposedly can only provide an orientation to the West. Now, after Tskhinvali, we are face to face with the fact that it was all a lie. There is no common system of values. There are Western, American, Russian, Chinese, Iranian, and Indian systems of values. And they interpret the simplest things differently — for instance, the genocide of peaceful citizens.

Accordingly, from a value point of view we will now take events as separate cases. Henceforth there must not be any demagoguery about the universalism of values, no projects in Russia of the supporters of "World Government," no propaganda plays insisting that the West is the unconditional and sole landmark on the path of our development or that "Russia is a European country." If we are a European country, then the West is "non-European" and we deprive it of the right to call itself Europe and spout geographical nonsense.

It is much easier to draw a different conclusion: Russia is an independent Eurasian civilization. Our value system is unique: in it, the mass murder of peaceful Ossetians is a crime, which we categorically will not tolerate. Having understood what position the Western countries took in relation to the tragedy in Tskhinvali, we finally answered the question whether Russia is a European country. It cannot be one, if European countries struck up a consensus relating to the events in Georgia, calling us the "aggressor" and the perpetrators of the genocide "innocent victims."

We Defended Our Interests — Hence, We Are Strong

Interests. Did Russia defend its interests in South Ossetia and Abkhazia? We must say that it did. This was not the primary thing, not the main thing, but nevertheless, it happened. Yes, we defended our interests before the face of those who wanted to assert their own at our cost. That is, we acted faultlessly in all regards, defending both our values and our interests. From the point of view of a system of values, we hope for understanding from other participants of the international process, since far from everyone in the world recognizes and supports American double standards. Everyone should take the defense of our interests as an accomplished fact and proof of our power. There is no need to justify this; it should simply be noted. On the other hand, we showed that the logic according to which only American interests must be equated with universal values, while everything that opposes them is "criminal," is finished.

In Tskhinvali, we defended our values and our interests and behaved precisely as an independent civilization, inasmuch as only a civilization can work out a system of values. In Georgia in August 2008 not only was there a demarcation line drawn distinguishing us from the US and its supporters on the level of interests, which is secondary; we also completely uncovered an irresolvable conflict on the level of values, which is the main thing: a conflict between us and them.

The End of Westernism in Russia

Who are those on the other side of the barricade? They are those who altogether recently were still thought of as "carriers of universal values." If we argued with them earlier on the level of interests, saying that we do not want to give up our position on some such question, now the conflict with the West takes on a completely different, deeper and more qualitative character (which, by the way, enlivened our society and formed our politics in the course of our entire national history in one or another form). Now is the very time to finally dispel the illusion of the universality of the West. The situation is more than favorable, since in my opinion nothing ended in Georgia. This is only the start of a fundamental conflict that will encompass the most diverse spheres of life, social, political, economic, cultural, and possibly even military. Thus, since everything is only beginning, it is exceedingly important for us to be aware that in Tskhinvali, the idea of the universality of Western values was buried for Russia. Henceforth we will relate differently to the format of international politics.

The experience that we paid for with our blood in Tskhinvali will open our eyes to many things: to the relation of the West to Iran, to the relation of the West to Syria and North Korea, to Palestinian autonomy, to China. We will begin to perceive many things entirely differently. The hypnosis of "World Government" has ended. The hypnotic suggestions of our Westernizers, our fifth column, no longer work. We can no longer refer to people who after the events of Tskhinvali defend universal values as lost. They are traitors. It is possible they erred, holding such a position before what happened, but now they must answer for it. They must be outlawed. There were people who welcomed Russia's seizure by Napoleon or Hitler. There were Vlasovs who went to Hitler's side, but we know what was done to them. I want to remind you of the Ribbentrop-Molotov Pact, in other words, the non-aggression pact, when the Soviet leadership had illusions about the possibility of peace with Nazi Germany. But after the 22nd of June

1941 these illusions were dispelled and Germanophiles, supporters of the friendship of the USSR with Germany, simply could not remain. So, too, in our times. Before the 8th of August 2008, we could have Westernizers, but after this date they can longer legitimately exist.

APPENDIXES

Alexander Dugin on Martin Heidegger

Interviewed by Michael Millerman
Nov. 3, 2015

Which period of Heidegger's thought do you find most relevant politically, and why?

The middle period of his life: the thirties and early forties. Before and after, he was less engaged in political philosophy. The reason for that is the following. Heidegger was an opponent of communism and liberalism. His attitude toward fascism was nevertheless very special. He rejected some crucial points of Nazi ideology: racism, materialism, modernism and technology (*Machenschaft*). So, we can deduce from his writings an implicit political ideology, a kind of meta-political draft that could be developed (which Heidegger himself did not do) into a sort of Fourth Political Theory. He touched on most explicit aspects of this meta-political draft in the thirties and forties, but on the margin of his work — in sketches for lectures, diaries and so on. He affirmed that any philosophy bears political philosophy in itself, as in the case of Plato. So, he mentioned some political ideas and concepts during Hitler's regime but didn't develop them. After 1945, there was a total destruction of Third Way politics, but Heidegger saw the Fourth Political Theory as an anti-liberal and anti-communist position that was critical vis-à-vis Nazism from the inside and not from the outside. Such criticism was possible only when Nazism was present. After its end he kept a silence that was very logical. He could not accept the critique of Nazism from the outside, from a liberal or communist point of view, so he stopped to express any political remarks.

Are there political lessons to be learned from *Being and Time*? Or from Heidegger's later thought on technology and *Gelassenheit*?

Any philosophy is pregnant with political philosophy. The politics is implicit in the philosophy. So I argue that it is quite legitimate to propose a political reading of *Sein und Zeit*, as well as of any other work by Heidegger. But in order to do that we need to understand sufficiently all his philosophy, including his less political first period. The question of technology (*Machenschaft*) is a continuation of the middle period concerns that were much more openly political. I would like to point out that *Gelassenheit* is a term that played an essential role in German mediaeval mysticism (Meister Eckhart and so on) up to Münzers Anabaptism. But I haven't done sufficient research concerning the possible political application of this idea.

Have you had the opportunity to read the Black Notebooks that have been published so far? If so, what did you find most interesting in these texts?

I have attentively read all three volumes of the Black Notebooks. The texts are very exciting, as are all lines belonging to Heidegger. I consider him the best philosopher of the West, so any word uttered by him is precious and demands careful meditation. But almost all the ideas formulated there I have met already in other writings. There is nothing special — it is Heidegger immersed in his thought. For the specialist in Heidegger there are many new interpretations of main topics and some brilliant aphorisms, but *Beiträge zur Philosophie* and *Geschichte des Seyns* as well as other writing of the thirties are more or less centered on the same problems.

One theme in the Black Notebooks is Heidegger's critique of the metaphysical presuppositions of mainstream National Socialism, presuppositions that he thinks Nazism shares with communism and liberalism. Is it possible to develop a political movement that is not based on metaphysics, but instead is open to the question of being?

In the Black Notebooks Heidegger has said nothing new concerning National Socialism that we wouldn't know or that wouldn't be a part of National Socialist doctrine. We should not forget that up to 1945 Heidegger was a member of the party, so being honest he should share the main points of the party doctrine. The inner criticism of National Socialism is effectively present in the Black Notebooks but it is not the main or central theme. In all three big volumes the space dedicated to the political topic is less than ten pages in whole. Not much. But in effect there are some important remarks in the Black Notebooks that show inner criticisms of the Third Political Theory in the sense of the Fourth Political Theory, which we need to examine with great attention. National Socialism is one of three political ideologies rooted in Modernity. Its totalitarianism is absolutely modern (Hannah Arendt has shown that). Heidegger was the most radical critic of Modernity as the oblivion of Being. He denounces the modern aspects of National Socialism, including racism. That is quite logical. And I share these criticisms.

In "The Age of the World Picture," at least in the form of the text that was published after the war, Heidegger rejects both nationalism and internationalism. Is there a third alternative, in your view?

He rejected nationalism not after the war but always, because he was a European thinker and continued the mission of the Western Logos. But the destiny of Logos was Greek in the Beginning and German in the end. That is an absolute fact — it doesn't depend on whether we are Germans or not. I accept this evident truth, being Russian. So the real Fatherland for Heidegger was philosophy and Germany as the nation of philosophers and poets — Hölderlin, Rilke, Schelling, Hegel, and Nietzsche. Nationalism is a modern, artificial concept, as is internationalism, which is its correlate. I am against nationalism and against all creations of modernity. I am deeply persuaded that Modernity is absolutely wrong in every respect. I agree with Heidegger that the Earth [*Erde*] in the *Geviert* [the Fourfold] is a philosophical idea, as is world [*Welt*] (or heaven [*Himmel*]). So Germany is an idea, as is Russia. Earth is dialectically linked with the Sky. And their battle (*Streit*) forms the Dasein of a concrete people (*Volk*). So Heidegger founded an existential understanding of people (*Dasein exiestiert völkisch*, he used to say) that is neither nationalist, nor internationalist. This point is the basis of the Fourth Political Theory.

How would you describe Heidegger's relationship to the Greeks? How did his relation to the Greek beginning of philosophy affect his stance toward the contemporary world? Do you consider it politically important to reflect on this Greek beginning?

We cannot understand the meaning of the End (where we live) without understanding the meaning of the beginning. All Greece — philosophy, language, culture — is of absolute importance. We are living on the margins of Ancient Greece. Everything was discovered and lived there already. European history is a weak and increasingly decadent repetition of Greek patterns. Political philosophy as philosophy in general was the creation of the Greek genius. The Greeks are our destiny, our identity. The Beginning is more important than the End, because the End is contained in the Beginning — not vice versa. So contemporary Europe is the End of the Greek in many senses.

In his writings of the 1930s, Heidegger attacks "liberalism" in a very expansive sense as a mode of thinking as part of the

history of being, with roots in Platonism and endpoints in the western European Enlightenment, including modern science as well as socialism and liberalism as ordinarily understood. He describes this larger liberalism as grounded on a notion of being that is eternal, universal, and without a fixed place in historical community. In your work, you advocate a "fourth" political theory that goes beyond liberalism, communism, and fascism. Do you agree with his being-historical understanding of liberalism, and if so, what, if anything, do you think he got right or wrong in the actual politics he engaged in during the 1930s? How would you correct or expand upon his ideas?

Being an admirer of Heidegger, I nevertheless have a personal vision of Platonism and Christianity that doesn't quite coincide with Heidegger's. But his criticism of liberalism is quite correct, because liberalism is the very essence of Modernity. The individual taken for the central point in this political ideology is the utmost interpretation of the Cartesian abstract (i.e. un-rooted) subject, brought to the last consequences. Communism and fascism as well have their ground in the Modern subject — collectivistic in communism and nationalist in fascism (racist in Nazism). I accept the existential and *Seynsgeschichtliche* criticism of liberalism proposed by Heidegger. The human being should be relocated historically and spatially, because the Da of Da-sein indicates a concrete phenomenological realm — a landscape, a language, a history. National socialism was wrong to accept modern concepts — of the individual, the race, the nation, the modern interpretation of the State, technology, progress, and so on. So there is no need to make appeal to it [National Socialism] in order to combat Modernity or liberalism. We need not imitate the contingent circumstances of the twentieth century, but try to found the Fourth Political Theory based on the pure intuitions of Heideggerian philosophy. Heidegger's criticism of liberalism is absolutely authentic and relevant, and we need to explore further the philosophical foundations of such criticisms, setting aside his political commitments.

A profound feature of Russia's own historicity is Christianity, specifically in the form of the Orthodox Church. But did Heidegger come to see all Christianity as a feature of the nihilistic history of being, a form of Platonism that calls to what is supposedly universal in human beings? Is Christianity compatible with your understanding of a politics grounded in Heidegger? Does the Russian Orthodox Church present an alternative to the western conception of a liberal Christianity, and how so?

That is a difficult question. I rather disagree with Heidegger's understanding of Platonism and Christianity. But I think nevertheless that we can propose a reading of Heidegger that wouldn't be incompatible with open Platonism (with the stress on the Dionysian side of it — especially of Neo-Platonism) and with existentially interpreted Christianity. Heidegger's friend and disciple von Hermann thinks that Heidegger's thought can be applied to Lutheranism. I have developed this difficult question in some of my works on Heidegger, such as *Martin Heidegger: The Possibility of Russian Philosophy* and *Martin Heidegger: The Last God*.[18]

In the *Contributions*, Heidegger writes that philosophy is always the philosophy of a people, and that a people is a people not on biological or racial grounds, but as a result of its own unique approach to the question of the meaning of being. You seem to share a view of peoplehood as rooted in fundamental questioning, but in your other writings, such as *Etnosotsiologia*,[19] you discuss what a people is in cultural-anthropological, rather than ontological terms. Did Heidegger

---

18 These are not yet available in English. The Russian editions can be purchased at http://www.evrazia-books.ru/. *Martin Heidegger: The Philosophy of Another Beginning*, is published in English by *Radix*.

19 http://www.4pt.su/en/content/ethnosociology-prof-adugin-lecture-1-introduction.

overstate things when he rooted peoplehood in inceptual thinking? Is a people bound together primarily by the fundamental questions they ask, rather than by diet, dress (costume-custom), political friend-enemy divisions, access to land and resources?

The ethnosociological approach is different from purely philosophical Heideggerianism. They don't coincide, but they don't exclude each other either. I agree fully with Heidegger's interpretation of "peoplehood" in political philosophy and in his philosophy as such. But in the field of ethnosociology we are obliged to deal with concepts of a different nature. Ethnosociologically, the people (Greek λαώς, German *Volk*) is the *ethnos* with a historical consciousness. There are *ethnoses* without it and artificial societies that have broken ties with their ethnic base. Heidegger is interested exclusively in the people defined by the possession of a philosophic Logos, who can therefore exist historically. Ethnosociology deals with different types of societies, where to be a people is but one of numerous possible kinds. So there is no contradiction, but rather a difference of theoretical standpoint.

Is history is really the history of metaphysics? Why should we privilege a philosophical account of history (that history is the history of being) over, say, an economic one, or one that focuses on minor incidents, accident, and chance?

History is a semantic sequence. Philosophy is concerned with the realm of meanings; so only philosophy deals directly with history, with its essence. All other approaches to history are mediated. We can suggest an economic explication of history, but to do that we first need a firm philosophical explanation of the economy. Accident or chance does not exist. Such names designate only the phenomenological fact that we don't know or don't want to seek the reasons, the meanings, and the ends of events.

What most distinguishes your reception of Heidegger from other receptions better known in the West, like Jacques Derrida's and Richard Rorty's, for instance?

Derrida put Heidegger in a New Left context and explains him in a postmodern way, thus perverting the main structure of his thought. As a liberal, Rorty is absolutely inadequate to deal with Heidegger, because their basic ideological situations are opposed and his interpretation of Heidegger is a caricature. In order to understand Heidegger correctly, we need to share the basic anti-modern position that explains the main direction of his thought. He cannot be understood by liberals or communists (new leftists). They will criticize him or pervert his thought.

What is the main thing that Heidegger scholarship or post-Heideggerian political thought has failed to grasp in Heidegger? And why has it failed?

First of all, it is almost impossible to understand Heidegger from a position fully exterior to his own, from the outside. After the end of WWII, in the West the liberal approach became the normative ideology and in the communist East obviously the communist one did. So an objective understanding or, better, empathic comprehension of Heidegger's (always implicit) political philosophy was excluded from very beginning. Liberals and communists (or their various mixtures) could criticize Heidegger or denounce him. Or else they could recuperate fragments of his philosophy, perverting the whole in a liberal or Marxist context. But acceptance of some aspects of Heidegger by Sartre, the French New Left, or postmodernists can be valid in nothing if we really want to understand his own thought. The same thing usually happens in liberal readings: severe criticism or rare efforts of recuperation. We understand nothing in Heideggerian political thought. Moreover, we have no means to understand it, or even to start trying, under the condition of the dominant post-WWII ideological landscape. It is not a failure; it is the result of historic paradigmatic conditions. We could start to understand Heidegger only after liberation from the hypnosis of all three forms of political Modernity — liberalism, communism and fascism. It is a challenge for the future.

The American pragmatist Richard Rorty read Heidegger as a resource for social democratic politics. He rejected Heidegger's being-historical story as anti-democratic, dangerous, and authoritarian, but drew on his destruction of the tradition of metaphysics as something that could help teach us that our vocabularies are contingent, that there is no final or total vocabulary, that there is neither God nor any substitute for God, like Reason, Essence, and so on. In short: Rorty used Heidegger in the service of political positions he already held. To what extent is your reading of Heidegger, which Rorty and those like him would regard as too far "to the right," in the service of previous political convictions, and to what extent has reading Heidegger transformed your previous political convictions and given rise to a new conception of what politics is and what it makes possible?

This is a complex question. About Rorty I have explained earlier. His pragmatist liberal American reading is very superficial, indeed. Heidegger rejected liberalism and mocked pragmatism, calling them Planetär-idiotismus. Planetary-idiot Rorty's reading of Heidegger is quite idiotic, as is fitting. It has no value at all in understanding deep Heideggerian thought. It is ridiculous.

As for myself, I am not to the right or to the left. My standpoint is against Modernity, which I reject as antithetic to the truth, but whose dialectic I consider not as something casual but as the dialectical moment of the destiny of Logos. Left and right are essentially modern. So they have nothing to do with my comprehension of being in its political dimension. But my anti-modernism had two periods: early Apollonian (traditionalism) and later Dionysian. The latter corresponds to the discovery of Heidegger's political philosophy. This discovery has led me to the development of a Fourth Political Theory, based on an existential interpretation of the essence of "*das Politische*" [the Political] (using Carl Schmitt's term).

A Canadian political theorist has written the following about you: "Dugin's 'politics' are bathed in the swampy waters of mystical esotericism and occultism, and his root-and-branch rejection of liberal democracy likely owes far more to his spiritualist and theological or pseudo-theological commitments than to anything we would customarily understand as political or philosophical." What has been a bigger influence on your "politics," Heidegger (philosophy/political philosophy more generally), or traditionalism, theology, and the like?

The example of the Canadian political theorist you have mentioned is a clear sign of hysterical ideological propaganda based on low rhetoric suitable for television debates where everybody shouts, but quite inappropriate for academic discussion. "Swampy" liberal idiots behave themselves in pseudo-academic ways, attacking those whom they consider to be their ideological enemy. Liberty and democracy end where full loyalty to liberalism and democracy end. That is what I call the third totalitarianism. If you are not a liberal democrat, we will liberally and democratically annihilate you. OK. That is logical.

Concerning the balance of traditionalism and Heidegger in my political views, I have explained in the previous answer.

In one of your books on Heidegger [Vol. 3], you raise the possibility that there are a multiplicity of Daseins, and postulate that Eurasia is ontologically the place where and the question in which they can "congregate in one special, central point that should unite East and West, Heaven and Earth, the depths and the heights, South and North." At other times, you give the impression of being less concerned

with congregation than with elimination, at least as concerns Atlanticism and liberalism. To what extent do you wish to see the actors and ideas you oppose (US liberalism, especially) destroyed, and to what extent do you want to let them be, so long as they let others be?

Liberalism is not an ideology that can let the other be. It can propose to the other to live only if it is a liberal other or at least the other that is going (may be in distant future) to become liberal. The limit case is when the other, being not liberal at all, agrees in essential cases to follow the will of liberals. Otherwise, he is finished. Liberalism is part of exclusivist Modernity and Modernity is essentially totalitarian. There is open totalitarianism in Nazism. It is more open and radical in communism. The totalitarian (Modern) nature of liberalism, which was hidden and implicit during the periods of confrontation with two other more openly totalitarian Modern regimes, is now increasingly transparent and apparent. So we have no chances to create Eurasia, based on non-liberal and non-Modern tradition on the basis of Fourth Political Theory, peacefully with the cold indifference of the liberal Americano-centric globalist West. The West will immediately intervene and it intervenes now. So war is imminent.

Concerning the Eurasian dialogue between the East and the West in Eurasian… You have opportunely mentioned the multiplicity of Daseins — Western and Eastern (in reality the nomenclature is much subtler). The liberals' version of the present-day West with American hegemony and left-liberal culture as "adogmatic dogma" is the most extreme form of inauthentic existence. So the West today lives on the other side of its own Dasein, in the most concentrated point of inauthenticity, in the full oblivion of its identity. Eurasia and Russia awakening will awaken the real Western Dasein from sleep and the loss of Self. With Eastern Dasein or better eastern Daseins, the situation is quite different. They are also seriously damaged by Modernity and have sometimes turned into simulacra, but they are much more alive than Western Dasein, which is dying. So the Eurasia I dream of could one day turn into the existential ground for the meeting of these two families of Daseins — Western and Eastern. But what is important is not the fact of meeting but the event of awakening, and mutual help in the awakening.

In one of your Heidegger books [Vol. 3], you write: "What is the Angel of Eurasia? It is a certain topos (place - τόπος), the topos of the Angelic Council, of the dialogue of awakened Daseins. It is the center of humanity, the pole of a new anthropology, the anthropology of the New Beginning." What are the prospects for this vision of Eurasia today? Are the Daseins of the peoples of the world awakening? Which ones? How would we know? What would that look like?

It is a very pertinent question, resounding with my previous answer as well. Eurasia is, precisely, a philosophical topos. It is first of all a *Seynsgeschichtliche* reality and only then a geopolitical, political or economical one. So it is for me the land of New Beginning, nowhere land, the na-koja-abad of the Persian thinker Suhrawardi. It is the territory for awakening an *Ereignis*. That is the core of my own *Seynsgeschichtliche* vision of the historic moment. The rebirth of Eurasia is an eschatological and spiritual event.

Today, Eurasian people are in a profound existential sleep. But the logic of history put them in front of the dilemma either to awaken or die. That doesn't depend on will: the will is orientated toward self-destruction. But the turn (*Kehre*) is always possible. Where there is risk there is salvation as well, as Hölderlin used to say. So I defend the choice of salvation. It is my choice and I hope Russia's choice. We see signs of possible awakening in Russia through intermediary forms, such as the rejection of liberalism and American hegemony, and the search for identity. The same is true on a lesser scale for other Eurasian peoples. But I am sure the awakening will come all of a sudden. Being prepared by all human history, it will arrive quite unexpectedly. Such is *Ereignis*. It can last. It is the rift in the texture of the sleep-time of inauthentic existence.

In the *Contributions*, Heidegger distinguishes between philosophy and worldview. It seems clear that what he is doing or trying to do belongs first and foremost to philosophy, not worldview. You sometimes write and speak as a philosopher concerned with the kinds of questions that concerned Heidegger. But you also produce works of political theory, geopolitics, international relations, and so on, and you seem to be promoting not only a way of questioning, but a system, an "episteme," a movement—albeit an open-ended one. How do you see the relation between philosophy, theory, and ideology or worldview in Heidegger and in your own work? (Do you object to the claim that you are both a philosopher and an ideologue?)

Ideology and Weltanschauung, or worldview, belong to the realm of doxa (δόξα). They are sub-philosophical, because philosophy deals with the truth that is far above doxa. The main concern of philosophy is to understand the truth and to be in the truth or near the truth. The philosopher is the guardian of the truth of being, Heidegger used to say. So between ideology and philosophy there is not exclusion, but hierarchy. Philosophy first, ideology later. Doxa can never be really true. In the best case, it can be approximation of truth; in the worst case—farthest withdrawal from the truth. The first is orthodoxy, the second allodoxy, or the act of intellection corresponding to the other-than-truth, oriented wrongly. The Fourth Political Theory and Eurasianism, or Dasein-politics, or existential politics, are the names for philosophical orthodoxy. Modernity and its three political ideologies are allodoxy. They are wrong not in the sense that they are not true (all ideologies are not true), but in the sense that they point in the direction that has nothing to do with the truth, in the other direction, not the right one.

Would you accept the designation of being a Right-Heideggerian? Why or why not?

Absolutely not. I am simply Heideggerian, trying to be as close as possible to this greatest thinker in order to understand him better. I am neither right nor left.

In a chapter of this book, you say that the Eurasian episteme consists principally of theology, ethnosociology, and geopolitics, corresponding to spirit, soul, and body. Where does Heidegger fit in to this picture?

Heidegger is here the heart, the existential core, the relation to death of all these three levels of analysis.

You are sometimes regarded as an apocalyptic thinker. But apocalypse and the end of times can mean different things depending on whether they are interpreted within religious traditions or in terms of the history of being, with Heidegger. Are you an apocalyptic thinker? In what sense?

Yes, I am an apocalyptic thinker, because I see time as Revelation and the Endtime as the integrity of the Revelation. The beginning of time is already the end, because it installs finitude and limit in life, with life and as life. So time is apocalyptic in itself. Not only because it flows in the direction of death, but also because the end and Revelation are the real and only nature of time. Time reveals being, hiding it. When time reveals more than it hides, it ends. If it hides more than it reveals, it lasts. Religion is orthodoxy in the sense I have explained before. I am with Heidegger in the truth and in seeking the truth. I am a religious man in definition of the directions that should lead to the truth. Christianity (at least Orthodox Christianity) and Heidegger in my personal existence and thought are fully compatible.

You have written four books on Heidegger now. Are you planning more? What's next for you in your exploration of the possibility of Dasein-politics and the Seyn-Politische [Being-Political]?

I have added to these four books some important and relatively big chapters (overall more than three hundred pages) concerning early Heidegger, his transition to *Sein und Zeit* from Husserlian phenomenology, his interpretation of Aristotle (which impressed me so much), his reading of Leibniz and so on. Some of these new developments are dedicated to the political side of Heideggerian thought — for example, the existential ground of the State, the three Indo-European functions in society, gnoseological levels in the Heideggerian interpretation of Aristotle's rhetoric, and so on. Now I am working on the biggest work, *Noomachy*, dedicated to exploring the existential identities of different civilizations. This project is inspired by the idea of the multiplicity of Daseins (the Heideggerian influence is obvious). I have already published nine volumes. Now I am working on the tenth (dedicated to the Greek Logos). There should be four volumes more. Maybe I will resume a detailed exploration of Heidegger's works after *Noomachy*, or maybe it will be in parallel. Presently, there is a kind of international philosophical movement around the Fourth Political Theory. I am participating in it actively. The work on existential politics, Dasein-politics, is obtaining a collective dimension. Not only in Russia, where there is an established nucleus of Eurasian intellectuals exploring Heidegger with myself. There are groups in France (where the most important Fourth Political Theorist Alain de Benoist lives), Italy, Spain, Brazil, Argentina, Germany, Hungary, Serbia, Greece, Poland, Portugal — even the USA. Existential America is a very important place in the philosophical map of the apocalyptical world.

The Four Political Theories

A schema of a model typology of the four political theories.

Pre-M:	Pre-Modern
M:	Modern
Post-M:	Post-Modern
Romanticism:	The artificial renewal of Pre-modernity
?:	Cannot be classified in terms of the three paradigms (pre-M, M, post-M) + Romanticism

1-5:	points of definition of Alexander Dugin's philosophy of politics
6 – 18:	points of nomenclature of Dmitri Kitsikisa classification of political theories (inserted by him for the description of the "third political theory") [Le national-bolchevisme (Nantes: Ars Magna Editions [Les Documents], 2006.)]

THE FOUR POLITICAL THEORIES

		1PT LIBERALISM	2PT COMMUNISM	3PT FASCISM/NAZISM	4PT
1	Subject	The Individual Bourgeois	The Class	The State *Race*	*Dasein* ?
2	Object	Privatized fragmented alienated atomic cosmos **M**	Socialized fragmented alienated atomic cosmos **M**	Living surroundings Romantically understood world **Romanticism**	Magical plastic medium Regime of water **Romanticism?**
3	Time	Present ephemeral progress **M**	Future progress **M**	The past and the future Cycle **Romanticism**	Eternity The vertical time of neo-Platonism (προοδεc/epistrope) ?
4	Space	Materially demarcated **M**	Materially merged **M**	Vital Space Vitalism **Romanticism**	Sacral space **Pre-M**
5	Type of State	From national state to global civil society **M**	From socialist state to global Communist society **M**	National state **M** Racial empire ?	A global sacral empire of the End ?
6	Attitude toward the concept of class and the meaning of peasantry	Overcoming the peasantry Farming Village capitalism **M**	Overcoming the peasantry Proletarianization Village industrialization **M**	Praise of peasantry Support village normativity **Pre-M**	Praise of the peasantry Support village normativity for the masses **Pre-M**

	1PT LIBERALISM	2PT COMMUNISM	3PT FASCISM/NAZISM	4PT
7	Attitude toward private property (small and large), to monetary circulation, to the economic control of the state, and to the idea of the national bourgeoisie and economic autarchy	Sacred private property Flat tax Minimization of state control From the national bourgeoisie to the international Free trade Monetarism **M**	Rejection of private property Nationalization State control over the economy The Plan Closed economy World Socialism Communist economy Industrialism **M**	Small private property Restriction of monetary circulation State control over the economy National bourgeois economic autarchy **M**	Abolition of private property Natural exchange Suppression and destruction of the bourgeoisie Abolition of money **Pre-M**
8	Attitude toward the nation: reality objective or subjective? Egalitarian or chauvinistic nationalism? The nation in relation to the state	Nation is a subjective reality Civic nationalism with a transition to cosmopolitanism and a common world The nation is a product of the state and disappears together with it **M**	The nation is a bourgeois, political, and historically conditioned concept, connected with state Internationalism The nation dies together with the state **M**	The nation is an objective concept Nationalism Egalitarian and chauvinistic The nation coincides with the state/ (in Fascism) **M** The nation is more primary than the state (in Nazism) **Romanticism**	The nation is a subjective reality, the bourgeois kind is not historically necessary The nation must be dissolved No nationalism The nation and contemporary government are bourgeois aberrations subject to destruction **?**

THE FOUR POLITICAL THEORIES

		1PT LIBERALISM	2PT COMMUNISM	3PT FASCISM/NAZISM	4PT
9	Attitude toward democracy and political parties	Liberal democracy (freedom) Party-based parliamentary system Separation of powers **M**	Popular democracy (equality) Proletarian democracy (it is a dictatorship, after all) Against parties, or one party (proletarian, Communist) **M**	Organic (direct) democracy (brotherhood) One party (national party) or no-party system **M**	No democracy (the *demos* is evil like the oligarchy and tyranny) No parties at all Alliance Monarchy/Aristocrats/Politicians – as in Rome **Pre-M**
10	Attitude toward the political charismatic hero	Negative or functional (the reformer) **M**	Theoretically negative but in practice positive The personality as the expression of class history **M**	The praise of the highest personalities The charismatic leader as a form of the best leadership The national (*narodnii*) tribune Leader *condotierre* – "The *Führer* principle" **M**	The superman in the centre of the political system Tsar of the world The Radical Subject The direct rule of the non-person [*nechelovek*] **?**
11	Attitude toward tradition	Negative Gradual process The improvement of society **M**	Extremely negative Technoligization Technical progress The destruction of the old **M**	Positive in combination with technical progress Conservative revolution **Pre-M/ Romanticism**	Entirely positive Traditionalism a striving to construct Tradition in all its fullness Difference between inertial tradition and total Tradition (which is taken as the foundation) **Romanticism/?**

227

	1PT LIBERALISM	2PT COMMUNISM	3PT FASCISM/NAZISM	4PT
12 **Attitude toward the individual and society**	The individual is primary and absolute Society is secondary and consists of a combination of individuals **M**	Society is more primary than the individual The individual has a class-based nature **M**	Holism Ontology of the whole The state is more primary than the individual **Pre-M** The race is more primary than the individual **?**	A total negation of the individual as a phenomenon Reorganized spiritual society as a holistic whole alongside the vertical heavenly fire The Radical Subject Superman **?**
13 **Attitude toward equality and hierarchy**	Equality of opportunity Material inequality **M**	Complete material and social equality **M**	Social equality Heroic meritocracy National inequality **M** Racial inequality **M/?**	Material equality Spiritual inequality Hierarchy of the soul Thearcy Telearchy Platonic castes **?**
14 **Attitude toward women**	Equality with men on an individual basis **M**	Equality with men on a class basis **M**	The glorification of women Nordic feminism Heroic virility **M/Romanticism**	Transcendent sex Spiritual feminism Heroic virility **Romanticism/?**
15 **Attitude toward religion**	Individual matter of each person Loss of public religion Evolutionism **M**	Atheism Historical materialism Evolutionism **M**	Religiosity of society Attraction to paganism and religious pluralism **Pre-M**	Radical theology New Metaphysics Traditionalism as a common obligation The religious paradigm of Neo-Platonism **?**

THE FOUR POLITICAL THEORIES

	1PT LIBERALISM	2PT COMMUNISM	3PT FASCISM/NAZISM	4PT
16 Attitude toward the philosophical concepts of rationality and irrationality	Rationality M	Proletarian materialistic rationality M	Irrationality Pre-M	Super-rationality ?
17 Attitude toward intellectualism and elitism	Partial acknowledgement on a class basis Bourgeois elitism on terms of openness of access for all (who is rich enough) M	Complete negation Elitism Proletarianism The intellectual is in the service of the class M	National education Negation of individualistic intellectualism Populism New aristocracy Romanticism	Hyper-elitism Hyper-intellectualism Philosophers rule The *paideia* for the nation (Ethnic Code – Eternal Return) The *paideia* for the elite (epistrophe, contemplation, return to the source) Romanticism/?
18 Attitude toward the Third World	Colonization Modernization Integration The West as the model M	Support Liberation from Western control Socialist development of Communism Pre-M	Against the West Inspired by the East Evola in Italy Inspired by Aryans and Hinduism in Germany **Romanticism** ?	Inertial tradition is better than all forms of modernity, but worse than integral, total Traditionalism ?

OTHER BOOKS PUBLISHED BY ARKTOS

Virginia Abernethy	*Born Abroad*
Sri Dharma Pravartaka Acharya	*The Dharma Manifesto*
Joakim Andersen	*Rising from the Ruins*
Winston C. Banks	*Excessive Immigration*
Alain de Benoist	*Beyond Human Rights*
	Carl Schmitt Today
	The Ideology of Sameness
	The Indo-Europeans
	Manifesto for a European Renaissance
	On the Brink of the Abyss
	The Problem of Democracy
	Runes and the Origins of Writing
	View from the Right (vol. 1–3)
Armand Berger	*Tolkien, Europe, and Tradition*
Arthur Moeller van den Bruck	*Germany's Third Empire*
Matt Battaglioli	*The Consequences of Equality*
Kerry Bolton	*The Perversion of Normality*
	Revolution from Above
	Yockey: A Fascist Odyssey
Isac Boman	*Money Power*
Charles William Dailey	*The Serpent Symbol in Tradition*
Ricardo Duchesne	*Faustian Man in a Multicultural Age*
Alexander Dugin	*Ethnos and Society*
	Ethnosociology
	Eurasian Mission
	The Fourth Political Theory
	The Great Awakening vs the Great Reset
	Last War of the World-Island
	Political Platonism
	Putin vs Putin
	The Rise of the Fourth Political Theory
	Templars of the Proletariat
	The Theory of a Multipolar World
Edward Dutton	*Race Differences in Ethnocentrism*
Mark Dyal	*Hated and Proud*
Clare Ellis	*The Blackening of Europe*

OTHER BOOKS PUBLISHED BY ARKTOS

KOENRAAD ELST	*Return of the Swastika*
JULIUS EVOLA	*The Bow and the Club*
	Fascism Viewed from the Right
	A Handbook for Right-Wing Youth
	Metaphysics of Power
	Metaphysics of War
	The Myth of the Blood
	Notes on the Third Reich
	The Path of Cinnabar
	Recognitions
	A Traditionalist Confronts Fascism
GUILLAUME FAYE	*Archeofuturism*
	Archeofuturism 2.0
	The Colonisation of Europe
	Convergence of Catastrophes
	Ethnic Apocalypse
	A Global Coup
	Prelude to War
	Sex and Deviance
	Understanding Islam
	Why We Fight
DANIEL S. FORREST	*Suprahumanism*
ANDREW FRASER	*Dissident Dispatches*
	Reinventing Aristocracy in the Age of Woke Capital
	The WASP Question
GÉNÉRATION IDENTITAIRE	*We are Generation Identity*
PETER GOODCHILD	*The Taxi Driver from Baghdad*
	The Western Path
PAUL GOTTFRIED	*War and Democracy*
PETR HAMPL	*Breached Enclosure*
PORUS HOMI HAVEWALA	*The Saga of the Aryan Race*
LARS HOLGER HOLM	*Hiding in Broad Daylight*
	Homo Maximus
	Incidents of Travel in Latin America
	The Owls of Afrasiab
RICHARD HOUCK	*Liberalism Unmasked*

OTHER BOOKS PUBLISHED BY ARKTOS

A. J. Illingworth	*Political Justice*
Alexander Jacob	*De Naturae Natura*
Jason Reza Jorjani	*Artemis Unveiled*
	Closer Encounters
	Faustian Futurist
	Iranian Leviathan
	Lovers of Sophia
	Novel Folklore
	Prometheism
	Promethean Pirate
	Prometheus and Atlas
	Uber Man
	World State of Emergency
Henrik Jonasson	*Sigmund*
Edgar Julius Jung	*The Significance of the German Revolution*
Ruuben Kaalep & August Meister	*Rebirth of Europe*
Roderick Kaine	*Smart and SeXy*
Peter King	*Here and Now*
	Keeping Things Close
	On Modern Manners
James Kirkpatrick	*Conservatism Inc.*
Ludwig Klages	*The Biocentric Worldview*
	Cosmogonic Reflections
	The Science of Character
Andrew Korybko	*Hybrid Wars*
Pierre Krebs	*Guillaume Faye: Truths & Tributes*
	Fighting for the Essence
Julien Langella	*Catholic and Identitarian*
John Bruce Leonard	*The New Prometheans*
Stephen Pax Leonard	*The Ideology of Failure*
	Travels in Cultural Nihilism
William S. Lind	*Reforging Excalibur*
	Retroculture
Pentti Linkola	*Can Life Prevail?*
H. P. Lovecraft	*The Conservative*

OTHER BOOKS PUBLISHED BY ARKTOS

Norman Lowell	*Imperium Europa*
Richard Lynn	*Sex Differences in Intelligence*
John MacLugash	*The Return of the Solar King*
Charles Maurras	*The Future of the Intelligentsia & For a French Awakening*
John Harmon McElroy	*Agitprop in America*
Michael O'Meara	*Guillaume Faye and the Battle of Europe*
	New Culture, New Right
Michael Millerman	*Beginning with Heidegger*
Maurice Muret	*The Greatness of Elites*
Brian Anse Patrick	*The NRA and the Media*
	Rise of the Anti-Media
	The Ten Commandments of Propaganda
	Zombology
Tito Perdue	*The Bent Pyramid*
	Journey to a Location
	Lee
	Morning Crafts
	Philip
	The Sweet-Scented Manuscript
	William's House (vol. 1–4)
John K. Press	*The True West vs the Zombie Apocalypse*
Raido	*A Handbook of Traditional Living* (vol. 1–2)
Claire Rae Randall	*The War on Gender*
Steven J. Rosen	*The Agni and the Ecstasy*
	The Jedi in the Lotus
Nicholas Rooney	*Talking to the Wolf*
Richard Rudgley	*Barbarians*
	Essential Substances
	Wildest Dreams
Ernst von Salomon	*It Cannot Be Stormed*
	The Outlaws
Werner Sombart	*Traders and Heroes*
Piero San Giorgio	*CBRN*
	Giuseppe
	Survive the Economic Collapse

OTHER BOOKS PUBLISHED BY ARKTOS

SRI SRI RAVI SHANKAR	*Celebrating Silence*
	Know Your Child
	Management Mantras
	Patanjali Yoga Sutras
	Secrets of Relationships
GEORGE T. SHAW (ED.)	*A Fair Hearing*
FENEK SOLÈRE	*Kraal*
	Reconquista
OSWALD SPENGLER	*The Decline of the West*
	Man and Technics
RICHARD STOREY	*The Uniqueness of Western Law*
TOMISLAV SUNIC	*Against Democracy and Equality*
	Homo Americanus
	Postmortem Report
	Titans are in Town
ASKR SVARTE	*Gods in the Abyss*
HANS-JÜRGEN SYBERBERG	*On the Fortunes and Misfortunes of Art in Post-War Germany*
ABIR TAHA	*Defining Terrorism*
	The Epic of Arya (2nd ed.)
	Nietzsche's Coming God, or the Redemption of the Divine
	Verses of Light
JEAN THIRIART	*Europe: An Empire of 400 Million*
BAL GANGADHAR TILAK	*The Arctic Home in the Vedas*
DOMINIQUE VENNER	*For a Positive Critique*
	The Shock of History
HANS VOGEL	*How Europe Became American*
MARKUS WILLINGER	*A Europe of Nations*
	Generation Identity
ALEXANDER WOLFHEZE	*Alba Rosa*
	Rupes Nigra

www.ingramcontent.com/pod-product-compliance
Lightning Source LLC
Chambersburg PA
CBHW020328170426
43200CB00006B/313